HELP KEEP OUR
PLANET GREEN

If you want grown-ups to recycle, just tell their kids the importance of recycling, and they'll be all over it.

—BILL NYE

MAKE GARBAGE GREAT

THE TERRACYCLE FAMILY GUIDE TO A ZERO-WASTE LIFESTYLE

TOM SZAKY / ALBE ZAKES

Foreword by JERRY GREENFIELD

HARPER
DESIGN

An Imprint of HarperCollinsPublishers

The best time to plant a tree was 20 years ago. The next best time is now.

—CHINESE PROVERB

CONTENTS

FOREWORD

MILLIONS of ice cream containers and wrappers bearing my name and image have been produced, sold, and discarded throughout the world. The ice cream contained in each package, and the pleasures it has brought to millions of people, were and remain Ben & Jerry's product focus. It's also true that all of those packages ended up in a landfill or were incinerated, save for the glorious souvenirs that are decorating dorm rooms and trophy rooms around the world.

Ben and I created a company that is noted for its socially responsible practices, and we're proud of what we accomplished. We tried to buy the best ingredients locally, and from mission-driven producers, and we sought to give back to the community with a spirit of generosity. I've always been sensitive about caring for the environment. I knew that in the production of ice cream, in the manufacture of its packaging, and in the countless plastic and wooden spoons we distributed, a lot of additional waste was generated (all the more reason to eat your ice cream on a cone!). I thought of these impacts as necessary, even when operating in the most thoughtful way possible.

My perspective changed once I read an advance copy of *Make Garbage Great*. I find the book an inspiring introduction to the journey of how many of our goods get to us, and where the products and their packaging go when we're done with them. The factoids are fascinating to me, and the infographics enticing. I am learning things about our individual and collective contributions to a garbage problem that, in simplest terms, is absurdly wasteful.

Garbage is the fossil of our consumer-driven economy. You can tell a lot about recent human history by looking at different levels of a landfill. I say "recent" because we didn't have so many disposable items until a few decades ago. Ice cream goes back a long way, but it was sold in reusable containers. Convenience, price, and our garbage systems foster an "out of sight, out of mind" blissful ignorance. We have come to accept the "consume, use, and toss" mentality as normal and sustainable. It isn't, and, thankfully, it is starting to change. Believe it or not, there's often more waste generated in creating a product or package than through its disposal. The current economic model of "extract, manufacture, and waste" results in a huge global waste problem; if you only look at the "fast-moving consumer goods" sector, about 80 percent of the $3.2 trillion material value is lost every year.

Most of us are sheltered from the environmental and human impact of our everyday decisions and lifestyles. We are bombarded with messages of consuming more, and we respond by purchasing things that we may or may not need. The positive side of this challenge is that as consumers, we are uniquely positioned to stem and reverse the tide of garbage. It begins with understanding the waste system, a fairly weighty topic that fortunately is conveyed in quite an engaging fashion in the book.

I was at first surprised to find that *Make Garbage Great* was produced as a coffee table book. What is wonderful is that the format allows the content to be savored in small doses; it allows us to not only learn about waste but also how to purchase, reuse, and discard differently, all the while entertaining. I am a sucker for that. There are 21 do-it-yourself projects in the book. My favorite is how to make a bird feeder from a used plastic bottle and a few used plastic spoons.

You probably already know that reusing and recycling are much better for the environment than landfill or incineration. You probably don't know that almost EVERYTHING is recyclable (from candy wrappers to pens, toothbrushes, and cigarette butts)—it's just cheaper to discard the old, and make and sell anew. Cheaper? Yes, to the manufacturer, and thus to the consumer at the time of purchase. But there are hidden costs of discarding our waste (as compared to recycling it), costs that show up in polluted waterways and water tables, in the air we breathe, and thus result in illnesses and related medical expenses that someone at some time has to pay for.

You'll read about lots of solutions, and some of the progress being made to make otherwise nonrecyclable waste recyclable. If the goal of this book is to inspire people to open their eyes about what they (and we collectively) waste, and to see how a little effort can make a world of difference, the authors have succeeded.

Tom and Albe are two of the leaders of Terra-Cycle, a company that recycles nonrecyclable products and packaging in over twenty countries. TerraCycle gets manufacturers to "sponsor" national collection and recycling programs for waste streams they create. Anyone can sign up for free. Brands use marketing dollars to pay the shipping and recycling costs; they are rewarded because many customers patronize businesses that reduce the consumers' footprint. These guys have shown that recyclability is a consumer priority (and have gotten companies to subsidize it). Millions of individuals and organizations throughout the world participate in their programs. Their passion for transforming our relationship to waste is infectious.

It will take a large-scale shift in assumptions, incentives, and practices to alter the deeply embedded global patterns of waste. My own fresh thinking about this challenge and opportunity has been jumpstarted by this book. Enjoy the ride.

JERRY GREENFIELD
COFOUNDER, BEN & JERRY'S
BURLINGTON, VERMONT

INTRODUCTION

WHAT IS GARBAGE? It could be simply described as "something that is worthless, unimportant, or of poor quality." However, another way to look at it is that garbage is anything that you are willing to pay to get rid of. Whether it's in our taxes or if we pay our garbage hauler directly—in fact globally we pay tens of billions of dollars to make sure our waste is quickly whisked away out of sight and out of mind.

In a traditional economy, products and services are traded because they have positive economic value; this is why it would sound absurd if a clothing factory started paying its consumers to take their T-shirts. However, that is exactly what happens in the world of garbage. In many cases that same clothing manufacturer generates T-shirt waste in the factory; many times perfect-looking garments that may have been simply overproduced are discarded. And if these garments end up in the Dumpster at the end of the day then the aforementioned absurd idea is exactly what the manufacturer will end up doing—paying to have his T-shirts taken off his hands.

By no means is this happening on a small scale. In 2010, the U.S. was generating 3.8 million tons of garbage every day. That's expected to hit 6.6 million tons per day by 2025. At this rate, and if nothing is done about it, we will be generating 12 million tons of garbage every day by 2100.

Historically this is a fairly recent phenomenon, perhaps only a century old as a concept. Before we were the advanced industrial civilization we are today, people made products out of materials that nature could easily decompose and put back into the cycle (cottons and leathers for clothing, wood for furniture, and metals for tools). Today those very same products are made from complex man-made materials that nature doesn't yet have a solution for (nylon and polyester for clothing, various plastics and composites for furniture, and plastics and rubbers for tools). To compound this, folks in the past had to covet durability to compensate for the lack of mass production. Replacing something wasn't as simple as shopping online or going to a nearby store. People would pass items down from generation to generation, and even fix them, instead of buying new disposable goods. If something broke, it got repaired by hand. Today if something is scratched or not perfect we often just throw it out and buy a new one.

By the 1950s, products like plastic-packaged food and disposable cutlery were transforming the way we look at and consume most things. Durability was no longer necessary, as plastic made new replacements cheap. It was just a matter of throwing the product away and going to the store to buy a new one. And in parallel we moved to bigger homes, drove larger cars, and measured our success by how many physical possessions we owned. A new age of garbage had begun.

Between the 1950s and today, companies like Walmart and Target began opening department stores with incredibly low prices for goods; suddenly the middle class could enjoy a lifestyle previously only afforded by the wealthy. Single-use disposable products and convenience foods skyrocketed in popularity. Home-cooked meals morphed into prepared microwaveable dinners.

Companies also started realizing that if they created products with shorter lifespans in mind, they could make their products with less cost and have them replaced more often, both of these driving increased volumes of consumption and growth in the global economy. The ever-shortened fashion cycles also ensured that line of clothing, or trendy electronic, might go out of fashion next season. Today, electronics with only minor improvements over their predecessors may enter the market semiannually.

HOW TERRACYCLE BEGAN

The idea for TerraCycle came to me in 2001, when I decided to take a road trip to visit my friends in Canada. I had ended up going to Princeton University, in New Jersey, and was getting a bit homesick. Up in Montreal my friends had been growing some indoor plants, with very little success, until one day they started feeding them worm poop. That is, taking organic waste from their kitchen, feeding it to red worms, which would then excrete vermicompost, or worm poop. This magical black substance turned out to be exactly what the dying plants needed, and the proof was there, before my eyes.

It was an amazing idea to me, as organic garbage was something we typically put in our trash and in turn pay someone to remove from our homes. Within months of this trip my friends and I had written a business plan for "The Worm Project" (later renamed "TerraCycle") and had constructed a massive prototype machine that would convert one ton of organic waste to amazing high-value worm poop every single day.

By the next semester I had dropped out of school to dedicate myself completely to Terra-Cycle; we even started packaging our (now liquefied) worm poop in used soda bottles, so as to have a product made from and packaged entirely from waste. The world took notice, and we were soon distributed in Walmart, Target, Home Depot, and other major retailers, showing that you can look at waste differently.

With this newfound perspective in mind we set our sights on any new waste stream we could get our hands on. Could it be reused? Today, TerraCycle collects millions of cell phones, ink cartridges, clothing, and toys that can easily be refurbished and resold. Could it be upcycled? From sewing juice pouches into backpacks to forming vinyl records into wall clocks, we found that the possibilities of upcycling were significantly bigger than we ever could imagine. And could it be recycled? In the following years our team of scientists at TerraCycle invented cigarette-butt recycling, chewing-gum recycling, and even developed a highly efficient way to recycle dirty diapers.

What makes something recyclable (or upcyclable or reusable) is entirely economics. Today, aluminum is widely recycled, not because of some unique technical wonder, but because the value of aluminum is so high that it offsets the costs of collecting and processing it and then some, leaving enough profit to attract a whole host of companies to get into the business of recycling it. But most other things, from pens to chip bags, are not recyclable, not because they can't be, but because it costs more to collect and recycle the product than the resulting materials are worth. So these things, once they become waste, end up in our trash destined for a nearby landfill or incinerator.

To solve this problem, at TerraCycle we have focused on finding various stakeholders that help make the nonrecyclable nationally recyclable. Many large consumer product companies have funded TerraCycle's Brigade® programs, where you can sign up to collect specific types of hard-to-recycle waste, get free shipping, and in some cases a donation per piece of waste to a school or charity of your choice, all courtesy of companies that are trying to make their packaging or product nationally recyclable. By 2014, through this model, 60 million people were collecting billions of pieces of waste across 25 countries.

Beyond our Brigade programs, cities from New Orleans to Vancouver have funded Terra-Cycle to bring citywide recycling programs to their citizens. Factories have joined the program using TerraCycle's waste innovation to recycle factory waste that would otherwise end up in landfills. Even consumers have been willing to help by purchasing our Zero Waste Boxes, in which they recycle everything from plastic gloves to cosmetics.

To eliminate the idea of waste we need to reflect on two things: how it comes to be and what we do with it once it's here. The first is tied directly to what we buy, so buy smarter and buy less. The second is tied to seeing waste not as a problem but something of value. Through this lens we can continue to advance as a society, while being more sustainable for the future generations that will inherit our planet.

WHY WRITE A BOOK ABOUT GARBAGE?

We want to change the way people look at garbage. In the natural world, waste isn't a problem; it's an opportunity. But since humanity is evolving at such a fast rate, and the amount of and kind of waste we produce can't be handled by nature, we must look to ourselves for the answer.

From elementary school classrooms to Fortune 500 companies, we've noticed throughout our travels that people don't know much about waste, as it's intrinsically something we want to get rid of and not think about. *Make Garbage Great* is our way of addressing this in a fun, easy-to-understand, and inspirational way. You'll learn about the history of all major waste categories, from thousands of years ago to today. You'll see amazing artwork and sculptures made out of things you once called garbage. You'll even be able to see how some of your favorite consumer products are manufactured.

You'll get tips on how to help, from making conscious purchasing decisions for your family to fun do-it-yourself projects using upcycled waste that will change the way you see garbage.

Garbage needs to be talked about, questioned, and analyzed on a fundamental level. We need people to be concerned and share this with their friends. Too many of us are unconsciously living in a disposable world, not aware of the harm and undue pressure it puts on the environment. This book is our attempt to spark these conversations.

Tom Szaky
Founder, TerraCycle

Page 2: Compressed automobiles ready for shredding in a junkyard. // Page 4: Shredded office paper. // Opposite: Aerial view of an expansive forest cut down by timber harvesting.

> If I were a tree, I would have no reason to love a human.
> — MAGGIE STIEFVATER, *The Raven Boys*

About 802,000 tons of #1 (PET) plastic bottles (water and soda, for example) were recycled in the U.S. in 2011. In the same year, more than two times that amount, about 1.9 million tons, were thrown out.

CHAPTER 1

PLASTICS

Human beings manufacture nearly 200 billion pounds of plastic every year. To really grasp that figure, consider these facts: there are also about 200 billion stars in the Milky Way and approximately the same number of galaxies in the entire universe. Think about how often you are exposed to plastic in some form every day. Plastic is in your toothbrush and dental floss, your Styrofoam cup of morning coffee, the gum you're chewing, the cigarette filters you step on while walking down the street, and the smartphone you can't put down. Pick up the nearest object to you at this very moment. Chances are there's plastic in it somewhere.

Previous spread: An over-
flowing landfill partially
filled with recyclables;
PET plastic beverage
bottles ready for recycling

(*inset*). // Above: An
upcycled TerraCycle U.K.
logo made from food and
beverage pouches.

It's hard to imagine how life would be without
this magical, lightweight, cheap material: no
more prepackaged food from the supermarket.
No more toys for the kids. No more convenient
bottles of water from the vending machines. From
its impact on our increasingly stuffed landfills to
wildlife's exponentially growing death toll, human-
generated plastic waste has evolved from a boon of
technology and materialism into one of the biggest
threats to the environment in human history.
The scariest part is that large-scale manufacturing of modern plastic products only began in the
1950s. How did our obsession get out of control so
quickly?

EARLY PLASTIC MATERIAL

Plastic is actually what's known as a hydrocarbon
polymer, or a substance that contains long, repeat-
ing chains of hydrogen and carbon atoms. The
earliest known human use of any type of hydrocarbon polymer can be traced way back to the ancient
Mesoamerican civilizations in Central America,
around 1600 BCE. What a groundbreaking day it
was for the ancient Mesoamerican who first discovered the Panama rubber tree *(Castilla elastica)*!
A source of natural latex resin, this tropical tree
enabled early Central American civilizations to
make rubber balls for a popular handball-like sport
called ōllamaliztli. Mixing the latex sap with juices
from a morning glory resulted in a stable, bouncy
wad of rubber, a precursor to plastic. Mayans,
Olmecs, and Aztecs all played variations of the ball
game, and it wasn't uncommon to find impeccably
painted murals or altars to the gods nearby.

There is a difference between rubber and
plastic. While rubber usually has a higher elastic-
ity, both are polymers composed of long hydrocarbon chains. This means that while they may
come from different natural sources, plastic and
rubber are extremely similar on a molecular level.
While today we consider rubber and plastic wholly
different materials, rubber is historically the
ancestor to all plastics. It would take another 3,000

A 60-watt light bulb could be powered
for six hours with the energy saved by
recycling one #2 (HDPE) plastic milk jug.

PLASTIC SYMBOLS

Plastics are usually categorized in seven different ways, depending on the plastic resins used to manufacture them. You see these numbers and letters on plastic products, enclosed within a small triangle that looks like a recycling symbol. But beware! This symbol does not mean that it is a recyclable plastic. Here is a complete breakdown of these plastic identifier codes (PIC) and what they really stand for.

 PET OR PETE (POLYETHYLENE TEREPHTHALATE)

Examples: water bottles, peanut butter containers, salad dressing bottles

Description: PET is most commonly used for bottled food and beverage products because it is light, transparent, and flexible.

 **HDPE (HIGH-DENSITY POLYETHYLENE)**

Examples: milk jugs, cereal-box bags, detergent containers, butter tubs

Description: HDPE is usually dyed or opaque, is flexible, and maintains very high strength considering how light it is.

 **PVC (POLYVINYL CHLORIDE)**

Examples: shower curtains, cleaning product bottles, building tiles and siding

Description: PVC is a rigid, strong, and resilient plastic used often in construction. When heated, PVC can release toxic chemicals into food it comes into contact with.

 **LDPE (LOW-DENSITY POLYETHYLENE)**

Examples: grocery bags, plastic sheeting, squeeze bottles

Description: LDPE is known for its high flexibility, so it is often the plastic of choice for disposable bags and squeeze tubes or containers.

 **PP (POLYPROPYLENE)**

Examples: plastic bottle caps, reusable plastic dishware, straws

Description: PP is a heat- and chemical-resistant, strong, hard plastic that won't crack when bent. More municipal recycling programs are accepting PP because it is a nontoxic, versatile plastic with many applications.

 PS (POLYSTYRENE)

Examples: Styrofoam, disposable rigid plastic cups, CD cases

Description: PS is an extremely lightweight plastic that can be turned into a white foamlike material great for insulation.

 **OTHER (VARIES)**

Examples: "biodegradable" plastics, nylon, DVDs and CDs, electronic-device casing

Description: Plastic that doesn't fall into PIC categories 1 through 6 end up in this catchall category. It's hard to say exactly what type of plastic a #7 is unless noted on the packaging, making this one of the most difficult-to-recycle categories of all.

A ski jacket can be insulated with plastic fiber made from five recycled #1 (PET) bottles.

Manufacturers have long chosen plastic for their products on the basis of price and functionality. But creating a more sustainable relationship with plastics will require a new dexterity on our part. It will require us to think about the entire life cycle of the products we create and use.

—SUSAN FREINKEL, *Plastic: A Toxic Love Story*

TEN THINGS YOU DIDN'T REALIZE ARE OFTEN MADE OF PLASTIC

1 **Cigarette filters:** cellulose acetate

2 **False teeth:** acrylic or synthetic resin

3 **Airplanes:** carbon fiber plastic composite

4 **Swimming pools:** fiberglass

5 **Flags and banners:** nylon or polyester

6 **Wire insulation:** PET, PVC, PP, and more

7 **Hip replacements:** PET

8 **Wall and ceiling insulation:** fiberglass

9 **Lumber:** PET, HDPE, or LDPE

10 **Movie screens:** vinyl

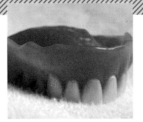

By 2030, the Lego Group hopes to completely switch over to using a sustainable plastic resin to make its eponymous Lego toys.

Opposite: A common sight at landfills: recyclable and organic materials that will no longer break down properly. // Above: It might not look that way, but false teeth are made from plastic resins. // Above, right: An iconic example of how plastic became so popular, the Lego.

years for humans to discover that hydrocarbon polymers in raw materials like tree resin and oil can be turned into the plastics that we know today. The first breakthrough came when Eduard Simon, a German apothecary, accidentally stumbled upon polystyrene (the material used in disposable utensils and Styrofoam) in his lab in 1839. Simon had taken resin from a tree, similar to the sticky sap of the Panama rubber tree, and distilled it. He noticed a few days later that the resin had unexpectedly solidified into a mysterious substance he dubbed styrol, which today we know as polystyrene. Because polystyrene had only been discovered accidentally and plastics had never been used, there were no applications at that time. However, Simon had unwittingly started a chain reaction of discovery and innovation that would, in the coming decades, grow into a global industry, making plastics one of the most widely used materials in our society.

PLASTIC IS INVENTED

While Simon was the first to discover plastic in a lab, British chemist Alexander Parkes was the first man to intentionally create a synthetic plastic, which he humbly called Parkesine, in 1856. Parkesine was meant to be a substitute for ivory, but Parkes's business went bankrupt before he was able to find any commercial success. Fourteen years after his discovery, American inventor John Wesley Hyatt acquired Parkes's patent for

DRINK POUCH COIN PURSE

Drink pouches are made of a durable material that lasts a long time. Rather than discarding them after one use, upcycle them into this simple coin purse that will hold your change, and help change the way you think about garbage at the same time. For kids ages 6 and up with adult supervision.

WHAT YOU NEED

/ Drink or food pouch
/ Self-adhesive Velcro® fastener
/ Scissors
/ Ruler
/ Pen or permanent marker

By 2014, more than 250 million drink pouches were collected and sent to TerraCycle for recycling. Send us yours for free; go to terracycle.com to find out how.

0

1

Cut off the top of the drink pouch and clean the inside with soap and water.

2

Measure 2 inches up from the bottom of your pouch and mark. Then, cut two slits down the seams on both sides from the front, top of your pouch. Be careful to cut through only one layer. Then cut straight across to remove the portion that you just cut.

3

Trim off the corner edges of the flap. Then, fold the flap over the front, crease it, and open it back up.

4

Attach the Velcro® fastener to the inside top of the flap. Fold the flap down and attach the other side of the Velcro® at the bottom of the pouch.

100 BILLION

Parkesine and developed a process for turning it into what we know today as celluloid. It was a great material to use in photography and movie film, and it is what most ping-pong balls are still made out of today. For the first time in history, a completely man-made, multiuse, durable plastic material had been fashioned in a lab. As the market for this material with many applications began to grow, a burgeoning plastics industry began to grow, too.

By the end of the nineteenth century, in the midst of the second Industrial Revolution, people were starting to recognize the viability of plastic as a replacement for many of the more expensive, difficult-to-collect raw materials. The process of thermoforming plastic — heating it so it can be molded—started to become a popular method of manufacturing plastic products. Thermoforming made manufacturing immeasurably more efficient and simple and is still in use today. Sheets of plastic are heated so that they can be molded into various shapes such as bottles, containers, and other products. It's a relatively simple process, and manufacturing goods with it is uncomplicated.

At the turn of the twentieth century, Ransom Olds, the founder of Oldsmobile, patented an early version of the assembly line, which in turn was perfected by Henry Ford in 1913. Production time for Ford's Model T decreased from more than a day to less than two hours, making cars less expensive and more accessible to everyday people. If an

Above: A chandelier made from upcycled 35-mm movie film at TerraCycle's headquarters in New Jersey. // Below: An early Ford factory production line, c. 1913.

entire vehicle could be manufactured cheaply and in only a few hours, one could only imagine what the future would hold for the mass production of consumer products.

The seeds of mass production and consumption were planted, but not long after were shaken by the Great Depression. After the stock market crashed in 1929, an explosion of unemployment, falling income, and struggling company profits crippled the purchasing power of consumers

FOOD WRAPPER NAPKIN RING

Food packaging serves up the perfect material for these fun, origami-like folded napkin rings. You'll need about three packages of a standard-size chip bag to create this project. Single-serving sizes work fine, too, as long as they're at least four inches tall and you're able to collect eight or more. For ages 8 and up.

WHAT YOU NEED

/ Plastic food packages (3 to 8 packages per ring)
/ Ruler
/ Scissors
/ Pen or permanent marker
/ Glue stick

Start with clean plastic food packages. Then cut your food packaging into 1¾-by-4-inch rectangles. You'll need 16 pieces to make a 2-inch-diameter napkin ring.

Take one wrapper and fold it in half lengthwise with the printed side facing out. Open it back up.

TIP: ONCE YOU HAVE THIS NAPKIN RING PROJECT MASTERED, YOU CAN ADAPT THE WOVEN TECHNIQUE AND CREATE BRACELETS, HEADBANDS, AND MORE.

Run your glue stick along the inside of the wrapper. Fold both sides of the wrapper in to the centerfold line.

Run your glue stick along the folded side of the wrapper. Then, fold the wrapper in half lengthwise again, so it is now a narrow rectangle.

5

Fold the wrapper in half width-wise and open it up. Fold both ends in toward the centerfold line. Refold along the center line. Repeat steps 2 through 5 on the remaining cut pieces.

6

Now take two folded wrappers and slide the two tabs from one piece into the slots of the other. Repeat this step linking all but one of your folded pieces.

7

To finish your napkin ring, open your last piece up, so that it is only folded in half widthwise. Loop the woven chain into a circle, so that the last two open ends are on top of each other. Push this piece through the two open ends. Then, tuck the two ends into the center of this piece.

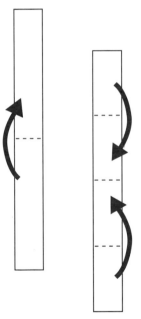

FINISHED

Every single day Americans throw away 570 million pounds of food wrappers and packaging.

around the world. With such a dismal economic outlook, the last thing on people's minds was what new products they should buy. The demand for consumer goods plummeted.

PLANNED OBSOLESCENCE

Real estate broker and author Bernard London came up with a drastic solution to the economic crisis in 1932. His theory, dubbed planned obsolescence, called for the government to attach regulated lifetimes to consumer products. Consumers would be forced by law to dispose of and replace any products past their government-mandated lifetime, theoretically stimulating the economy due to an increase in spending and an artificial surge in demand. While planned obsolescence was never enacted in any official capacity, the concept was attractive to consumer-product industries. Manufacturers realized that if they could intentionally design a product to have a short lifespan (for a variety of reasons), consumers could be deliberately driven into purchasing more products more frequently because they would perceive them as unfashionable, outdated, or less functional. It's an effective marketing scheme; just think about how many people line up for the newest version of the iPhone, only to line up again

a few months later for a slightly more updated version. The newest has become an indisputable commandment of consumption, so much so that our purchasing habits have been contorted into an incessant craving for new things that we can throw away mindlessly because we think they can always be replaced.

EVERYTHING PLASTIC

The 1930s and 1940s catalyzed our understanding of what we now consider the modern consumer mindset. In 1938, businessman and inventor Earl Tupper developed Poly-T, a durable plastic material made from oil refinement waste. Then, in 1941, chemists at a textile company, the Calico Printers Association in Manchester, England, patented polyethylene terephthalate (PET). This discovery led to the plastic beverage bottles and polyester clothing so ubiquitous today.

World War II had pushed consumer-centric industry aside in favor of industries necessary for wartime, such as steel and ammunition, but when the war ended in 1945, corporations began rebuilding a relationship with consumers who were once again starting to crave new products.

Left: TerraCycle's offices in Trenton, New Jersey, are made entirely from upcycled materials. //
Above: Oil rig.

When exposed to high temperatures, the plasticizing agents and phthalates used to make #3 (PVC) product packaging can actually leak into food or beverages and be toxic.

In 1946, Earl Tupper began production of his iconic Tupperware. His products were a breakthrough for homemakers everywhere, making storage hassle-free and keeping food fresher longer. Tupperware's introduction into the market foreshadowed one of the most prominent consumer-product revolutions in history: the age of disposability. Not only could plastic be made in massive quantities for little cost, but also the material was developing an ever-growing catalog of possible applications.

On the heels of an October 1947 *House Beautiful* magazine feature article entitled "Plastics . . . A Way to a Better More Carefree Life," consumers began to look at plastic products as the way of the future. The magazine depicted plastic as the ultimate answer to the prayers of housewives everywhere, making life in a postwar society easier than ever before. One picture in the article showed kids drawing on plastic wallpaper, only to be effortlessly cleaned off by Mother who was smiling beside them. Disposable products like plastic cutlery and dishware made home life immeasurably simpler; when the family was done with supper, cleaning up could be a matter of sliding all of the dishes into the trash instead of washing them by

hand. With the advances in technology, cheap plastic grew more prevalent in the market year by year, and disposability was perceived as a real time-saver, a great thing.

An onslaught of innovations and technological advancements hit society like a tsunami in the 1950s. In 1951, high-density polyethylene (the plastic every milk jug is made from) was synthesized by the Phillips Petroleum Company. In 1954, polypropylene, now found in everything from packaging to textiles, was discovered. Toys like the Barbie doll and Legos, and household goods such as Saran Wrap, the messiah of leftovers everywhere, are only a few of the consumer products brought to market during this time.

People of all socioeconomic statuses could now afford similar things, as plastic became a standard for production due to its abundance and low cost. In fact, the products were so cheap to manufacture and so readily replaceable that the need for long-term durability went out the window. This new age of consumerism revitalized that concept of planned obsolescence, with inventor Brooks Stevens defining the mindset of the era best when he said that it "instill[ed] in the buyer the desire to own something a little newer, a little better, a little sooner than is necessary." From the

Above: A Tupperware party. Tupperware products are primarily made with #4 (LDPE) and #5 (PP) plastics. // Right: A vintage Barbie from the 1960s.

PLASTIC BOTTLE BIRD FEEDER

This simple bird feeder is made from plastic spoons and a drink bottle. By filling the bottle with seed, even birds can get in on protecting the planet from trash. For ages 12 and up with adult supervision.

WHAT YOU NEED

/ Plastic bottle
/ Three plastic spoons
/ Twine
/ Birdseed
/ Marker
/ Hobby knife
/ Hot glue gun
/ Drill

0

1

Start with a clean and dry bottle. Use the marker to evenly space out holes at various heights for the three spoons to go through. Mark two holes on opposite sides of the bottle for each spoon. You should end up with six marks total.

2

Use your hobby knife to cut an oval hole in the bottle at the points that you marked, allowing enough space for the spoon to slip through.

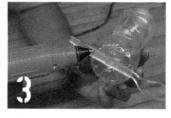

3

Slip a spoon all the way through the bottle. Be sure the hole is still big enough for birdseed to get through; if not, remove the spoon and make the hole bigger. Then slip the spoon back through and secure it into place with several dabs of hot glue. Repeat for the other two spoons.

4

Drill a hole into the bottle cap about the same diameter as the twine.

5

Run the twine through the cap, and make a thick double knot on the inside to ensure the twine can't pull through.

Fill the bottle with birdseed, preferably outdoors, as some birdseed will spill through the holes while filling.

Re-cap the bottle, and hang it from your favorite tree or post!

If one out of every ten #2 (HDPE) plastic bottles in the U.S. were recycled, nearly 200 million pounds of plastic waste would be diverted from landfills.

1950s onward, plastic evolved from mind-boggling revelation to standard necessity. It would go on to protect soldiers and law enforcement with bullet-proof clothing, thanks to DuPont's development of Kevlar material in 1965, and literally became a standard in 1969 when Neil Armstrong placed a nylon American flag on the moon's surface.

Plastic rapidly became a choice manufacturing material, as it was not only cheap to manufacture, but was also lightweight, could be made rigid or flexible, had insulating properties, and had a range of potential consumer uses. By 1980, polymers like PET became standards in food packaging, and plastic became the most produced material in the world.

THE PROBLEM WITH PLASTIC

Now take a step back from all this and ask yourself: Why does this matter? Plastic helped save our economy from collapse. It drives and stimulates our free market. It makes our lives easier and our products replaceable! What's the problem?

For the answer, take a look at the Great Pacific Garbage Patch in the Northern Pacific Ocean. Considered one of the largest landfills on earth, this swirling mass of plastic waste was formed by a current system called the North Pacific Subtropical Gyre. Segments of the patch have been estimated to be about the size of Texas (268,820 square miles), perhaps even larger, because much of the waste is located underwater. Ninety percent of the patch is comprised of plastic; it's like a giant, swirling toilet bowl of artificial waste that never goes down the drain. To make matters worse, there are five similar gyres like this in each of the planet's

A pile of plastic waste and garbage.

PLASTICS TIMELINE

1600 BCE Polymers are first used by ancient Mesoamericans, where naturally occurring latex is turned into rubber to make balls and bands.

1856 Alexander Parkes invents the very first man-made plastic "Parkesine."

1870 John Wesley Hyatt, a New York inventor, and his brother develop and patent the process for creating a new synthetic plastic: celluloid.

1913 Henry Ford develops the assembly line, increasing the viability of mass production across nearly all industries.

1941 Chemists at the Calico Printers Association of Manchester patent polyethylene terephthalate (PET), which has become one of the most widely used packaging materials in the world. Most beverage bottles are made of this material.

1839 CE Apothecary Eduard Simon accidentally discovers polystyrene (PS), and Charles Goodyear perfects vulcanization, a process that makes rubber more durable. Atop a mountainous landfill of plastic and old tires, we raise a disposable cup to you, sirs!

1872 Eugen Baumann produces polyvinyl chloride (PVC) for the first time.

1890 One of the first instances of thermoforming—heating plastic into a malleable material—is used to create rattles for babies. Manufacturing with plastic becomes a cheaper and more efficient method of creating consumer goods.

1932 Bernard London publishes his book *Ending the Depression Through Planned Obsolescence,* which suggests that consumer products should have government-regulated lifetimes.

1938 Earl Tupper turns waste from oil refinement processes into a new, durable plastic called Poly-T, and launches a consumer revolution with Tupperware.

1946 Tupper begins selling his new Tupperware products. Homemakers rejoice, as storing food and keeping it fresh become as simple as snapping on a plastic lid.

1947 *House Beautiful* publishes an issue with a massive section titled "Plastics . . . A Way to a Better More Carefree Life." Carefree for now . . .

PRE-1950

1954 Inventor Brooks Stevens repopularizes planned obsolescence.

1951 Tupperware is sold exclusively through the wildly successful Tupperware Home Parties hosted by housewives across America. Meanwhile, two American chemists find a catalyst that forms high-density polyethylene (HDPE), or what will make up your average milk jug.

1965 DuPont develops and unveils the bulletproof material Kevlar, made from synthetic fiber.

1979 For the first time, plastic production surpasses the production of steel.

2011 Americans generate 32 million tons of plastic, or 13% of the entire waste stream. Only 8% of that was recycled. Throwing stuff away is just easier, right?

TODAY Each year, we throw away enough plastic dishware and cutlery to wrap around the earth 300 times. Plastic is everywhere: in our dental floss, cigarette filters, electronics, toys, chewing gum, clothing, nail polish . . . the list is endless. To make things more frightening, plastics can take thousands of years to break down. This means that since the first synthetic polymers were developed in the 1800s, any plastic that hasn't been incinerated is still here. How's that for a reality check?

1953 Saran Wrap appears on store shelves everywhere. Before it started keeping our food fresh, Saran was used by the army to help ventilate combat boots.

1976 The almighty plastic becomes the most commonly used material in the world. Unfortunately for us, there are few ways to recycle it.

1980 Polyethylene terephthalate (PET) starts replacing paper in food packaging, making products cheaper and easier to manufacture, and last longer.

2000 Plastic makes up 24.7 million tons of the municipal waste in the U.S., up from 390,000 tons in 1960.

POST-1950: THE AGE OF DISPOSABILITY

major oceans, all of them a veritable aquatic trash heap.

Between 1960 and 2000, Americans alone went from generating around 400,000 tons of plastic in the municipal solid waste stream (what consumers throw in the trash) to 24.7 million tons. That's more than a 6,000 percent increase in the amount of plastic waste in the U.S. in only forty years. In 2011, that number skyrocketed again to 32 million tons, only 8 percent of which was recycled. We are endangering the long-term well-being of the planet because of a desire for short-term wealth and material objects; that polystyrene plastic fork from lunch, or the cellulose acetate cigarette filter flicked onto the sidewalk, or the junk computer monitor left on the curb—none of them will ever biodegrade. Most plastics will only break down if exposed to direct sunlight (photodegradation). When plastic photodegrades, it turns into smaller bits of plastic, called nurdles, so it never truly disappears, it only gets easier for a fish to swallow or for toxins like styrene to leach into groundwater and soil.

Because plastic is a man-made invention, it is useless to organisms and the ecosystems in which they reside, unlike all other natural waste produced in the environment. Plastic takes anywhere from thousands to millions of years to degrade into nurdles. If we are generating 200 billion tons

Left: E-waste, like these computer monitors, is one of the fastest-growing waste streams in the world. // Right: This map shows the two masses of ocean debris collectively known as the Great Pacific Garbage Patch. // Opposite: Corn is one type of plant that can be used to make plastic.

of plastic annually, it is safe to assume that we will quickly overstress our natural resources and overfill our landfills.

There needs to be a revolution, both in the way we look at plastic waste and in the ways we decide to act upon our materialistic desires. As a consumer, your decisions are what drive corporations to manufacture for disposability. We can replace a plastic cup or buy the new version of the iPhone, but we can't replace our planet. You are the solution the earth desperately needs.

PLASTICS TODAY

It's a misconception that there are unrecyclable plastics. Everything is recyclable; it's just a matter of finding someone willing to pay to do it. PET (water and soda bottles) and HDPE (milk jugs) (see Plastic Symbols, page 15) are widely recycled

WHAT'S THE DEAL WITH "BIODEGRADABLE" PLASTICS?

No petroleum-based plastics are biodegradable, and they never will be. If something is biodegradable it means that it can naturally decompose in the environment, a fact that is certainly not true of the petroleum plastics that pervade our lives.

Plant-based plastics, on the other hand, are a different story. These can be made with anything from corn to sugarcane and bark, all of which are sustainable resources. For example, polylactic acid (PLA) is often the bioplastic of choice for companies that manufacture biodegradable plastic cups, food containers, and other packaging. Polylactic acid is easier to make than other bioplastics because it is made from corn, a plentiful renewable resource. Some famous examples include the Frito-Lay SunChip bag and Stonyfield yogurt cups. Manufacturers first take dextrose (a type of sugar) from the corn and add bacteria, which turn the dextrose into a compound called lactic acid. The molecules of this compound then start linking

together into one long chain, similar to the process that turns oil byproducts into plastic. The end result is a new batch of corn-sourced plastic.

But just because plastic can come from a plant does not automatically mean that it will biodegrade. To make that happen, bioplastics must be disposed of carefully and correctly, otherwise they may end up being landfilled where they won't degrade just like any other plastic material. Most, like polylactic acid, have to be composted in very hot and humid industrial composters that are strictly managed and regulated. And forget about sorting and recycling bioplastics—as of now, there is so little of it on the market that no wide-scale recycling or collection efforts exist. In fact, if you mix even just one piece of bioplastic in with oil-based plastics, the recycled material can be contaminated, compromising the quality.

because there's a lot of material available and the recycled end products have a lot of applications. Most importantly, the value of the recycled product is higher than the actual cost of collecting and recycling it.

It's true that we run into recycling problems when products have multiple components (a container with a lid), or are complex products altogether (a laptop), as parts may be made with different resins. The cost of sorting and recycling is then higher than the value of what the actual recycled product would be. Nonetheless, there are many plastic products that are made of single

resins, yet we still recycle less than 10 percent of the plastic waste that ends up in the trash. Here's where 90 percent of plastic waste goes.

LANDFILLS
There are a whopping 1,900 landfills in the U.S. alone, and they receive more than 50 percent of all waste generated in the country. In the European Union, more than 60 percent of waste ends up in landfills. One of the largest landfills in the world, the Bordo Boniente landfill in Mexico, took on 12,000 tons of waste every day until it closed in 2011. Even so, people continue landfilling waste

there because no alternatives were ever put in place. In Paraguay, thousands of impoverished families live on top of or next to Cateura, the country's largest landfill, a common occurrence in developing countries.

Landfills consist of a base layer, usually clay, along with a layer of sheeting that functions as a liner to prevent the waste from leaching into the ground, and then alternating layers of municipal waste and earth. Plastic that ends up in a landfill is difficult to break down because it doesn't have access to sunlight and can't photodegrade (which is still bad for the environment anyway), so some plastic waste may spend hundreds, thousands, or millions of years underground. When it rains or when landfills are improperly managed, they can also leak toxic chemicals into the earth, polluting local groundwater in the process. They also release greenhouse gases like carbon dioxide and methane into the air as waste decomposes.

Even though they are horrible for the environment, landfills continue to flourish not only because they are a cheap form of disposal, but also because they can generate revenue. Landfills make money by charging waste management companies a small fee per ton of waste dumped, the keyword here being "waste." Landfills don't make big bucks through recycling, and neither do the waste management companies that haul garbage away to them. The more waste that exists, the more money there is in the pockets of the landfill owners and waste management companies.

OCEAN DUMPING

Dumping waste into the ocean is a very cheap method of waste disposal, with appalling effects on the ecosystem and marine life, yet it still happens. It wasn't even until the early 1970s that ocean dumping was banned by law with the enactment of the Ocean Dumping Act of 1972.

Human garbage, debris, and other pollutants that enter the ocean can wreak havoc on

Plastic Bank

IMAGINE A WORLD in which an impoverished community can earn money, health services, or tools for cleaning local beaches and waterways of plastic debris. The Plastic Bank, a social enterprise based in Canada, is trying to do exactly that.

Founded in 2013 by Canadian social entrepreneur David Katz, the Plastic Bank is a young and ambitious company trying to help end poverty while decreasing the amount of plastic waste in oceans and on beaches around the globe.

It works like this: Individuals or organized groups of people start collecting plastic debris around their local communities. The plastic waste can then be taken to a Plastic Bank location, where it is exchanged like a form of currency for home goods, tools, and even 3-D printed parts and products. The collectors leave with helpful products for themselves and their families, while the plastic they collected is processed and recycled. The recycled plastic, called Social Plastic™, can even replace virgin plastic, further lessening our dependence on new plastic sourced from petroleum.

The business model has yet to be fully tested, as the first Plastic Bank facility will open its doors in Peru by the end of 2014. To help ensure success, you can visit plasticbank.org and sign a petition for companies to start using Social Plastic™, the ultimate socially conscious plastic, to help raise demand for it. If enough of us start demanding that our products be made with socially responsible plastic, big business will have no choice but to sit down and start listening.

Plastic trash piled up in a waterway.

marine ecosystems. Containers or plastic bags of fertilizer, for instance, have been known to wash downstream into the ocean, spilling chemicals and other compounds into the water. Algae happen to love nutrient-dense material like this, so much so that they can proliferate to unsustainable levels, depleting the surrounding water of oxygen. There are around 400 areas of water like this all across the globe, places where marine life can't live.

Marine animals living close to human settlements are also at constant risk of injury or death because of plastic waste like shopping bags and packaging. Fish can easily mistake tiny bits of plastic for food, and can even get them stuck in their gills. Whales and turtles have turned up dead on the beach with hundreds of pounds of plastic bags in their bellies. Plastic six-pack rings can wrap around a marine mammal's snout, preventing it from eating or breathing. Any piece of plastic packaging, container, or wrapper that we use is a potential death sentence for an unsuspecting marine animal.

INCINERATORS

Incineration is a popular way to "deal" with waste around the world, especially because energy can, in some cases, be generated from the process. It's not surprising that the resulting pollutants from incinerating or combusting garbage can damage the atmosphere and the health of human beings. For one, when plastic and discarded rubber is burned, toxic chemicals like greenhouse gases, dioxins, and furans (both of which are known carcinogens) get pumped into the air, some of which are linked to cancer, reproductive issues, and hormone fluctuations in animals and human beings. Still, countries like Germany and Japan thrive on incinerating municipal waste because it's an easy, cheap way of generating energy.

Studies have indicated that waste incineration may put human beings at risk for a wide variety of diseases. A 2007 study published in the *Journal of Hygiene and Environmental Health* found that people living near a Portuguese waste incinerator had higher levels of mercury, lead, and cadmium in their blood. Another study, in a 2005 volume of the Polish medical journal *Medycyna Pracy,* found that individuals living near incinerators were at an increased risk of birth defects, thyroid and respiratory problems, and cancer. Waste incineration that is not well regulated by the government can also contribute to smog, much like the thick smog that

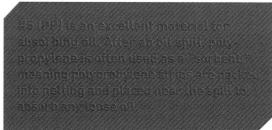
#5 (PP) is an excellent material for absorbing oil. After an oil spill, polypropylene is often used as a sorbent, meaning polypropylene strips are packed into netting and placed near the spill to absorb any loose oil.

Countless tons of waste wash up on shores worldwide every day.

plagues parts of China's industrial sectors. The smog is so dense in these regions of the country that it hangs in the air, limiting vision and making air purifiers a household necessity.

While there are many influencing factors, conventional wisdom would suggest that incineration, much like the burning of fossil fuels, is a major contributor to climate change, reductions in the ozone layer, and a global increase in respiratory diseases and cancers. And until the value of protecting the environment and our health outpaces the value of energy, things are likely to continue this way.

LOOKING FORWARD

At TerraCycle, we don't limit the scope of our efforts to any one waste stream, and neither should you. But the fact of the matter is, the ubiquity of plastic waste forces us to pay particular attention to it. We're not just referring to the huge gyres of floating plastic debris in our oceans or the faulty plastic identification code system (see Plastic Symbols, page 15) leading people to believe any plastic with a number on it is recyclable. The real issue is the plastic packaging and other products that consumers don't realize are made from or contain plastic.

Take just about any product packaging, for example. Chip bags, cookie snack bags, cheese wrappers, portable baby food pouches — these are all composed of plastic, and the typical consumer knee-jerk reaction is to throw them in the trash, possibly because their size makes them seem insignificant in terms of waste. It's exactly the reason why TerraCycle provides recycling solutions for product waste worldwide, from toothpaste tubes and glue bottles to dairy tubs and cereal bags, and much more. The packaging might

be upcycled or recycled into plastic pellets for manufacturing, diminishing the need for virgin plastics.

For less conventionally recycled plastic waste, we've developed an innovative recycling system that allows us to recycle waste like cigarette butts. The cigarette paper and leftover tobacco get composted, and the plastic filter is recycled into products like industrial shipping pallets. Nearly 1.7 billion pounds of cigarette butts are thrown away worldwide every year. That's about 4.5 trillion individual cigarette butts.

It's important to manage the plastic waste stream because the repercussions of inaction are dire. The more demand there is for virgin plastic, the more pressure we put on the market for unsustainable, nonrenewable resources like oil. Demand for plastic in general is driven by many factors, one

Below: TerraCycle's global offices, like this one in Toronto, Canada, are all made from waste.

// Opposite: A typical landfill with plastic trash everywhere.

Of all plastics thrown away in 2011, #4 (LDPE) plastics, like those in grocery bags and squeeze bottles, made up more of the municipal solid waste stream than any other type, representing more than 23% of all plastics in municipal solid waste.

LIFECYCLE OF A POLYSTYRENE FORK

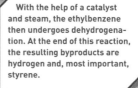

1 The life of our friend the disposable fork begins in a pool of thick, sticky crude oil located deep under the surface of the earth in an oil reserve.

4 Naphtha is then exposed to a process called steam-cracking, where it is heated and turned into even more components that, when combined and reacted together, form ethylbenzene.

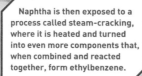

5 With the help of a catalyst and steam, the ethylbenzene then undergoes dehydrogenation. At the end of this reaction, the resulting byproducts are hydrogen and, most important, styrene.

7 The polystyrene pellets are then shipped, perhaps several thousand more miles, to manufacturers around the globe, such as those that make disposable cutlery.

2 Once the oil has been collected at the reserve, it is sent through a vast, complex pipeline system to an oil refinery, often thousands of miles away, for further processing.

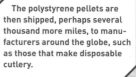

3 Now at a refinery, the crude oil is broken down through a process called fractional distillation into various components called "fractions." The most important fraction in plastic production, called naphtha, is collected.

6 Styrene is now produced in vast quantities, and the most important step of plastic production, polymerization, begins. Here, massive chains of styrene are chemically reacted together to form polystyrene plastic pellets. Some of the polystyrene will be used for rigid disposable cutlery, and some of it will be turned into expandable polystyrene, or Styrofoam.

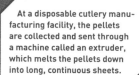

8 At a disposable cutlery manufacturing facility, the pellets are collected and sent through a machine called an extruder, which melts the pellets down into long, continuous sheets.

9 This malleable sheet of polystyrene can now be thermoformed into nearly any shape via injection molds. In this case, the plastic is injected into two-piece, fork-shaped molds.

10 After injection, the newly formed forks are released from their molds, cooled so they may harden, and are sent off for packaging and shipping.

11 Now a finished and packaged disposable fork, bulk quantities of the product are shipped to supermarkets, cafeterias, airlines, schools, and fast-food restaurants around the world.

12 Having traveled several thousand miles from its original home in an oil reserve, through a refinery, and down the assembly line of a plastic factory, the worldly polystyrene fork now sits proudly next to your Caesar salad from the mall food court.

13 After five or ten minutes of use, the fork that was birthed halfway around the world is tossed into the garbage. Welcome to your new life as garbage, little buddy!

14 The fork ends its long journey as a useful product by being turned into trash. Oh, the places it will go! Maybe it will end up being dumped on top of a mound of fetid, rotting garbage in a landfill, where, after being buried by several additional tons of garbage, it might sit for a few thousand years. Not only that, but it risks leaching styrene into the groundwater, perhaps even making its way into your cup of drinking water.

OR MAYBE it will find its way to a water source like a tributary or river, where a hungry beaver may mistake it for food and get it stuck in its throat. Even if on the off chance it gets broken down into smaller pieces, it may just end up finding its way into the stomach of a seagull where it will sit undigested. And where there's one piece of plastic waste in the environment, there are dozens, if not hundreds more. It's only a matter of time before that seagull's belly is so full of indigestible plastic waste that it dies.

There's always the chance that our friend the fork will be sent off to an incinerator to be combusted and turned into energy, or more accurately, toxic pollutants and greenhouse gases that are ejected into the sky.

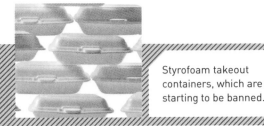

Styrofoam takeout containers, which are starting to be banned.

FIVE PLASTIC PRODUCTS EVERY FAMILY SHOULD AVOID

1 Microbead Soap: Face wash, soap, and body scrub products are often made with tiny little plastic pellets called microbeads, and they can easily get into our waterways. Lake Ontario alone was found to have 2.8 million of these plastic beads per square mile, and marine life can fatally confuse them for fish eggs, an underwater delicacy.

2 Styrofoam Containers: Cities and towns around the world are banning Styrofoam food containers, and for good reason: when heated, they can leach chemicals into foods and drinks. Styrofoam, or expanded polystyrene, can leach a chemical called styrene into hot liquids like tea, or food heated in the microwave. High quantities of styrene can actually even act as a neurotoxin to humans.

3 Products Containing PVC: Polyvinyl chloride is a common type of plastic, identified by a #3 and the letters "PVC." It can be found in many products like shower curtain liners, plumbing, and plastic school supplies like pencil cases. Vinyl chloride, used to make PVC, is listed as a known carcinogen by the World Health Organization and the EPA. Chemicals called phthalates are also commonly used to make PVC less rigid, but can interfere with hormone function in humans, especially children. As of 2009 in the U.S., phthalates have been banned in children's toys, but not in other high-exposure products like school supplies.

4 Disposable Dishware: While single-use plastic utensils and dishes make cleaning up a breeze, they are in fact some of the most wasteful products you can purchase. It's even been estimated that Americans use nearly 100 million plastic utensils each day, and considering these utensils are rarely recycled, most are destined for the landfill. Reusable dishes or cutlery made out of metal or ceramic are almost always the more eco-friendly option, as they can be reused for many years.

5 Bottled Water: Most developed countries have free access to clean water, yet people spend $100 billion on bottled water every year. It would be one thing if the majority of this consumption came from nations with limited access to clean water, but that's not entirely the case. The U.S., Germany, Italy, and France are all among the top per capita consumers of bottled water in the world. Even more water and energy is required to manufacture the plastic bottles themselves, which, of course, never truly break down.

of the largest being the purchasing habits of consumers. The more cheap and disposable products we want, the more dependent we make ourselves on plastic. It's that simple.

THE TOLL ON WILDLIFE

The garbage patch gyres in our oceans show how much of an ecological threat plastics are. Even more damning is that plastics didn't really exist in large quantities until around the 1950s, meaning that the most recent generations of human beings are directly responsible for this grave blight on the environment. Iconic images of turtles and fish with plastic six-pack rings around their heads

or torsos—these are real results and we are responsible for them. Birds, whales, crocodiles, and countless other animals have been found dead after consuming massive amounts of plastic bags and plastic debris.

Wildlife is being injured or killed and local ecosystems damaged and destroyed by the plastic predicament. When plastic at sea photodegrades, it breaks up into tiny pieces that are easily swallowed by marine life, slowly killing them. Things like discarded synthetic fiber fish nets can entangle and kill marine creatures, and plastic bags can be especially deadly when eaten by ocean dwellers. In 2002, a whale was found dead on the coast of France with more than 1,700 pounds of plastic bags in its belly, and turtles have been known to ingest plastic bags, mistaking them for jellyfish. Dead birds have even been discovered full of plastic debris they mistook for food. Because we use plastic products just about everywhere, the waste is found everywhere, too.

Clockwise from top left: Plastic bottle and resins. // Plastic litter is a huge health risk for wildlife. Here a pelican mistakenly tries to eat some trash. // This TerraCycle tote is made from used plastic bags.

A pregnant pitbull in 2013 was found dead in New York City with an intestinal blockage caused by a plastic object she had eaten; cows in India were known to consume plastic bags, disrupting the function of their stomachs, until the bags were banned in 2009; and seabirds have been known for years to sometimes feast on small plastic nurdles. These are only a few of the dozens of high-profile examples, not to mention the untold countless deaths in the wild that we don't know about.

WHAT YOU CAN DO

You are part of the solution we so desperately need. As a consumer, the power of the purchase is directly in your hands. While you can't always influence the buying habits of others, you can make smart decisions to help lower our dependence on plastic and drive demand for it into the ground. Source reduction is another way to put it,

FOOD POUCH TOTE BAG

Reusable tote bags are every eco-person's essential accessory. You can't get more stylish than creating a tote from sewing together colorful and durable food pouches—a perfect project for teens and adults. Here's how you can make your very own reusable bag, which will get the attention of all your tree-hugging friends! For ages 16 and up.

WHAT YOU NEED

- 27 drink or food pouches
- Webbing or grosgrain ribbon
- Thread
- Scissors
- Binder clips
- Sewing machine
- Clear tape
- Ruler

0

TIP: MIX AND MATCH COLORS OF POUCHES TO MAKE A TOTE THAT FITS YOUR UPCYCLED STYLE.

1 Start by cutting the tops off of your food pouches, then clean and rinse them out.

2 Lay out the pouches. For the front and back of the tote you'll need two panels that are three pouches wide by three pouches tall; two sides will be three pouches tall; and one bottom will be three pouches tall.

3 Overlap the pouches along the bottom row of the front panel by ½ inch. Tape on back. Continue overlapping all of the rows from the front and back panels in this same fashion.

4 Sew along each overlapped edge.

5 Then, overlap each row by ½ inch, creating your front and back panels of the tote. Tape in place.

6 Sew along the overlapped edge.

7 To create the sides and bottom of the tote, overlap three pouches by ½ inch along the short edges. Tape in place. Sew along the overlapped edge.

8 Create a double-turned hem by folding down the top edge of the front, back, and two sides of the totes by ½ inch. Then stitch along the fold.

9 Create your handles by cutting two 18-inch pieces of webbing or ribbon. Tape them about ¾ inch down on the front of the tote where the pouches overlap. Then stitch in place.

10 Trim the bottom panel so that it's the width of the tote.

11 With the wrong sides facing together, lay the bottom panel on top of the front panel. Clip together with binder clips.

12 Sew along the clipped edge. Repeat steps 11 and 12 for the back panel.

13 Place the side panel against the front edge of the tote and clip with binder clips. Sew along this edge, leaving ¾ inch opening along the bottom. Repeat this step for the remaining three sides.

Polycarbonate, one of the more common plastics labeled #7 (Other), contains the infamous endocrine disruptor bisphenol A (BPA), which can disrupt the function of hormones in human beings.

Enough. Man is capable of reform once presented with the facts, and the fact is that bottling water and shipping it is a big waste of fuel, so stop already. The water that comes to your house through a pipe is good enough, and maybe better.
— GARRISON KEILLOR, *The Salt Lake Tribune* (September 29, 2007)

Opposite: Ducks near garbage. // Clockwise: An upcycled logo made from cookie wrappers in TerraCycle's Toronto office. // A TerraCycle chair made from candy wrappers. // A small beaker of biodiesel.

and all it means is purchasing less materials and products that are made out of plastic. The materialistic attitudes coveted by the developed world are what led to this plastic "paradise" in the first place, and changing the way we think about the products we buy is the only way to stop it.

You can start by abandoning products like disposable plastic cutlery, cups, and plates, and instead invest in reusable, washable alternatives. Durability is the name of the game, as something that lasts years means years of new products you don't have to buy. The same goes for bottled beverages; stop wasting your money on plastic water bottles and simply refill a metal container over and over again. Refill stations (water fountains especially outfitted with spouts for refilling water bottles) are becoming more commonplace, so if you see one, use it! Spend the extra few dollars on durable products, so you won't need to replace them as often.

Plastic is very versatile, so before throwing it in the trash consider its other possible uses. Old

CDs, yogurt cups, vinyl records, and glue bottles are all just begging to be made practical again.

If upcycling isn't your thing, you can be a conscious steward of proper recycling techniques. Take a look at the plastic identification code on the underside of the plastic products you buy (see Plastic Symbols, page 15); if it's a #1 or #2, it's safe to assume you can throw it in the plastics bin headed to the municipal recycling center. Some centers accept other numbers, but always check to be sure. If resins are intermixed, the resulting contamination can render the entire batch of prospective recycled plastic useless.

Want to maximize on your recycling efforts, but don't know where to start? Check out the website earth911.com, where a nifty search function allows you to look up just about any type of waste or recyclable and where it can be recycled near you. Type in "plastic bags" and your zip code, and it'll generate a list of places near you that accept and recycle them. The side bar will even display recent news stories relating to the waste material you searched for.

Individuals can get the eco-movement mobilized on the ground, but we can't forget the nonprofits and other organizations that are out there to help us. A club of engineering students at Carnegie Mellon, Engineers Without Borders, partnered with the environmental nonprofit Reuse Everything Institute, Inc. to turn discarded plastic bottles into roofing in poverty-stricken areas in developing nations. Jobs are created, impoverished communities are improved, and plastic waste is given a use once again.

For-profit companies are a crucial piece of the puzzle as well, bringing innovation and capital to a problem that desperately needs both. An alternative energy company called Ágilyx has developed technology capable of actually repurposing plastic trash back into crude oil. It's not an endorsement of oil, but every gallon we can get from the plastic debris on the side of the road or floating in the ocean is one less gallon of virgin crude that needs to be collected.

Civilization as we presently know it is too dependent on plastic for any sweeping changes

Thousands of bottles were reused to create this eco-friendly roof.

Vinyl Record Coasters
6 pack

Stonyfield Farm
ORGANIC

lowfat
PLAIN
smooth & creamy

32 OZ (2L)

Clockwise from top left:
An upcycled CD clock
made by TerraCycle. //
Keeping the same tune:
TerraCycle also makes
coasters from old vinyl
records. // One of Terra-
Cycle's first partners was
Stonyfield Farm; here is
a prototype Crayon con-
tainer made from yogurt
containers.

to be made overnight, and big corporations and manufacturers are unlikely to spontaneously stop utilizing it to make their products. It's a realistic analysis, but it isn't as dismal as it might sound. Why? Because of you.

You decided to pick up this book, making an informed decision as an active consumer. The power, ultimately, lies with you. What you buy determines what is produced and sold. What you throw away in the garbage instead of recycling determines what ends up as useless landfill refuse. What you see as "trash" or "garbage" or "useless" continues to perpetuate the myth that some waste is simply not recyclable. You have an incredible amount of power at your disposal; you just have to be conscious of it.

CD ROOM DIVIDER

CDs had a good run in the past, but now they tend to be stacked up and go unused. Pull them out and give them another spin. Put the colorful printing on display or use silver-toned ones for a subtler, upcycled look.
For adults.

WHAT YOU NEED

- 185 CDs
- Tracing paper
- 500 plastic washers
- 325 (⅛-inch) rivets with ⅛-inch grip
- 125 (5/32-inch) rivets with ½-inch grip
- 70 feet (1 by ¼-inch) molding
- 4 (1½-inch) utility hinges
- 16 (½-inch) screws
- Paint
- CD room divider template (see page 46)
- Pencil
- Permanent marker
- Power drill
- ⅛-inch drill bit
- 5/32-inch drill bit
- 5/64-inch drill bit
- Scrap piece of wood
- Rivet
- Tape measure
- Screw driver
- Paintbrush

Start by organizing your CDs into stacks of 15. These will be used for the height of the room divider.

Trace over the template found on page 46 and cut it out.

Place the template on top of the CD and make a mark at each hole. Repeat for all of your CDs.

Drill into each CD at the point you marked with the ⅛-inch bit. Use a piece of scrap wood under your CD to avoid drilling into your table.

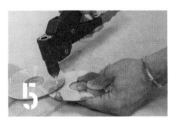

Overlap pairs of CDs matching up one set of holes. Place a plastic washer in between the overlapped holes to prevent cracking. Insert a ⅛-inch rivet into the holes and secure in place with the rivet gun.

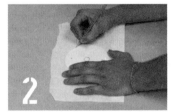

6

Continue step 5 connecting sets of 15 CDs together. You should make 12 sets total.

7

Take four sets of 15 CDs to make one panel. Overlap two of the sets. Drill into pairs of CDs placing a piece of scrap wood under the pair before drilling. Place a plastic washer between the overlapped holes. Insert a ⅛-inch rivet and secure in place.

8

Repeat this step until you have four sets of 15 CDs connected. Then repeat for the two other panels.

9

Cut the lengths of the molding into 12 (52-inch) sets. This will be the vertical part of the frame.

10

Continue to cut the remaining molding into 12 (14¼-inch) sets. These will be horizontal parts of the frame.

11

Paint the molding a color of your choice and let dry.

12

Line up the molding along the edges of one of the connected CD panels. Place the two smaller lengths of molding between the two longer lengths at the top and bottom of each panel. Do this for the front and back of each panel.

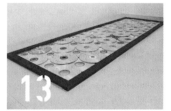

13

Have a friend hold the frame in a rectangle while you center the CDs on the frame.

14

Drill ⁵⁄₃₂-inch holes through the molding and CDs. Make one hole for each bordering CD ½ inch away from the inner edge.

CONTINUED →

15 Rivet the holes with the ⁵⁄₃₂-inch rivets. Repeat to finish your two other panels.

16 Line up the utility hinges with the corners of the frame and drill a hole using the ⁵⁄₆₄-inch bit.

17 Use the ½-inch-long screws to attach the hinges on opposing sides so it can unfold into a "Z."

FINISHED

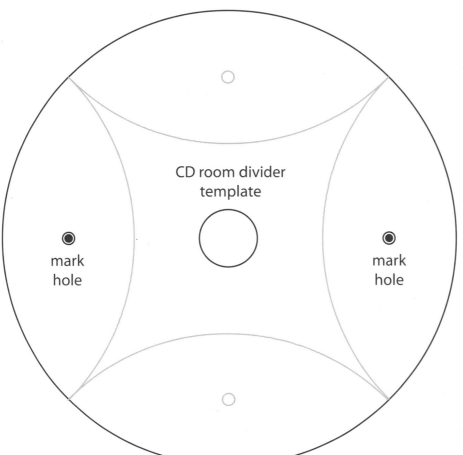

CD room divider template

mark hole

mark hole

TIP: EXPERIMENT WITH COLORS AND PATTERNS BY LAYING OUT YOUR CDS BEFORE YOU START RIVETING.

We humans have become dependent on plastic for a range of uses, from packaging to products. Reducing our use of plastic bags is an easy place to start getting our addiction under control.

—DAVID SUZUKI, ENVIRONMENTALIST

A beached sea turtle tangled in plastic fishing nets.

About 95% of all metal produced in the world is iron. This is due to its endless applications, as it is cheap and is used to smelt many other varieties of metals, like steel.

CHAPTER 2

METALS

How much steel do you think is used every year to sustain our industrialized world? A million pounds? A billion? Try more than 3 trillion pounds, and that's just one type of metal. In addition to steel, we are dependent on dozens of metals that are used to build everything from the tallest steel-reinforced skyscrapers to the tiniest electrical microcomponents in your mobile phone. Metals of all shapes and sizes keep our infrastructure in place and modern civilization from crumbling back into the Dark Ages.

Previous spread: Rusty metal pile. The inside of a metal factory (*inset*). // Above: Pallets of soup cans ready to be filled at a canning factory. // Opposite: A rusty steel railroad bridge.

Like plastics, all sorts of metals find their way into almost every facet of daily life. Every electronic device you touch, car you drive, or building you set foot in is at least partly composed of a metallic substance. Even most nonmetal products you consume each day are manufactured or packaged on an assembly line of automated machinery made of steel and iron. Metals of all sorts have had a major impact on the mass consumption that we all know and love, and their use continues to expand. Metals have provided us with many conveniences, making our lives easier and more efficient ever since we first stumbled upon them thousands of years ago.

METALS FROM THE BEGINNING

While there's still some uncertainty surrounding when metals were first truly "discovered" by early humans, copper was likely the first "utility metal" that actually made tools more durable and less prone to wear like their stone counterparts. Copper was being smelted in parts of the Middle East and Asia by 4500 BCE. Still, people would soon discover that copper could be made even stronger and more resilient, and it would only take another thousand years.

That breakthrough came about around 3500 BCE, when people realized they could combine copper with tin, making bronze. By now, Egyptians and other ancient civilizations began using bronze spears and other weapons. By increasing the amount of tin in the molten copper mixture, the resulting compound was harder and less brittle. The Bronze Age flourished for a few thousand years, bringing to some of the greatest ancient civilizations more durable tools and a greater capacity for technological innovation.

It would be a few thousand years before the next great leap forward in technology, when iron began to show up more frequently in the ancient world. It's hard to identify precisely when the Iron Age began, but the forging of iron had spread to western parts of Europe by 1200 BCE. Iron was especially important to early nations with little access to tin, a material required to manufacture bronze. Iron, on the other hand, was widely available in many regions. The ancient world had a new raw material with which strong tools could

A typical house contains more than 400 pounds of copper, in things like pipes and electrical wiring.

Steel can be used over and over again, retaining 100% of its strength no matter how many times it is reprocessed into new steel products.

be produced in quantity. And what did they do with it? Fight to the death, of course! Weapons were cheaper to manufacture, so just about any nation or empire could outfit an entire army at minimal expense.

The discovery of iron changed human civilization in profound ways after being discovered more than three thousand years ago. While it provided the fuel necessary to facilitate our insatiable bloodlust for conquering new lands, it also led to some of the most important advancements in human history. Farming was infinitely simpler with the use of iron tools for sowing and harvesting.

Once iron technology found its way across the globe, there were few large strides forward in metal production and use for several hundred years. Heavy cast iron (what your typical cannon ball is made of) was forged in Europe around 1150 CE, and iron continued to thrive as the perfect material for inflicting damage upon others, whether by sword or by siege. The next major advances came in the eighteenth and nineteenth centuries.

TWO INDUSTRIAL REVOLUTIONS

As the Industrial Revolution spread throughout the world in the eighteenth century, so too did

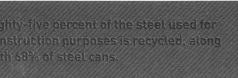

Eighty-five percent of the steel used for construction purposes is recycled, along with 68% of steel cans.

some of the biggest scientific and technological breakthroughs in human history. For one, forging iron became an incredibly efficient process. By the 1780s, a man named Henry Cort had optimized iron forging, pushing production up to 400,000 tons annually in Britain alone. Other scientists and inventors began to experiment with iron and other metals to see what other applications and uses they could develop. In 1800, Alessandro Volta fashioned an early version of the battery after noticing that certain metals could carry a current of electricity after being exposed to moisture.

The tin can was also patented around this time, proving to be an indispensable form of food

Copper is antimicrobial. Bacteria and other pathogens that come into contact with copper surfaces are readily killed, which is why many public places and other high-traffic establishments are built with doorknobs and handles made from copper alloys like brass.

Above: Steel workers using heavy equipment to construct a large steel structure. // Left: Humans have relied on metal for everything from tools to protection, shelter, and weapons for thousands of years.

TIN CAN OFFICE ORGANIZER

If you're looking for a fun and easy way to organize your supplies that is also eco-friendly, look no further than your recycling bin. Tin cans transform into fun receptacles for all of your art supplies with this great project for children. Pairing the cans with tissue paper adds a style that looks like it came off a store shelf, rather than being destined for disposal. For ages 6 and up with adult supervision.

WHAT YOU NEED

- 3 to 5 tin cans
- Tissue paper
- Scissors
- White glue
- Paintbrush
- Hot glue gun
- Scrap paper
- Markers (optional)

0

1

Start with clean tin cans. Cut your tissue paper so that it covers the height of the can. You can cut multiple pieces and overlap them.

2

Create a mixture of glue that is half water and half glue. Then, brush the glue mixture onto your can.

3

Arrange and attach the paper onto the can and let dry.

4

Brush another coat of the glue mixture on top of the paper. Affix your supply labels, if using.

5

Arrange your cans as you'd like and add a bit of hot glue to all of the points where your cans touch.

preservation. Once standardized, the tin can made it possible for perishable food to travel long distances, or sit on a store shelf for an extended period of time.

A huge revelation came about in 1824, when Hans Christian Oersted isolated aluminum for the first time. This was an important discovery: aluminum is one of the most common metals found in the earth's crust, but it is very reactive and isn't found in nature in its pure state. Oersted accumulated a very small sample of it, but proved that pure aluminum could actually be produced. People were so thrilled with the lustrous, shiny new metal that it was valued even higher than gold and silver for a time. As a show of glory and power, an aluminum cap was placed atop the Washington Monument in the 1880s. That's right: your aluminum soda can would have been like a brick of gold in the nineteenth century.

Following Volta's battery prototype came some of the biggest developments in electromagnet technology. In 1825, British electrical engineer William Sturgeon invented the first electromagnet by coiling a wire around an iron bar. Once an electrical current is introduced to the wire, a magnetic field is created, the strength of which can change based on the strength and flow of the electrical current. Today, we find electromagnets everywhere; when someone presses your doorbell, they are closing a loop of electricity and activating an electromagnet, causing a metal hammer to hit and ring the bell. When you turn on your toaster, you are triggering an electromagnet that radiates enough heat to toast your morning bagel.

The first half of the Industrial Revolution was coming to a close, soon to be replaced by a second. The first Industrial Revolution, which started in Great Britain in the late eighteenth century, was marked by a shift away from agriculture and toward urban industrialism. Factories were constructed, steam power was introduced, and iron and textiles started being mass-produced.

It was the first time that manual labor was starting to be replaced by more efficient

The supply of copper in the earth's crust is enough to last humanity for 120 million years at present levels of usage and consumption.

Clockwise from top: A spool of copper wire cables. // Men pouring molten metal c. 1930s/1940s. // Portrait of Alessandro Volta holding his battery invention. // Opposite: Metal factory.

Whenever we engage in consumption or production patterns which take more than we need, we are engaging in violence.

—VANDANA SHIVA, *Earth Democracy: Justice, Sustainability, and Peace*

About 98% of all iron ore mined on earth is used for steelmaking.

machinery, like James Hargreave's "spinning jenny" that could spin many spools of thread at once. Production was becoming more efficient than ever before, but still more improvements could be made.

That came with the onset of the second Industrial Revolution, which began in 1855 thanks to a British industrialist named Henry Bessemer. He developed a technique for turning raw pig iron, a brittle and less refined form of iron, into one of the most important industrial metals: steel.

STRENGTH OF STEEL

Steel costs more to produce than iron, but it is much more durable. Railways use steel for long segments of track; buildings use steel reinforcements and girders for more reliable support; and automated machines using steel components eliminate manual labor, lowering manufacturing costs. In this way, the second Industrial Revolution was like a global happening, with the worldwide expansion of railroad networks, telegraphs, automated machinery, and a quickly expanding global steel industry.

By the early twentieth century, steel was in such high demand everywhere that steel magnate Andrew Carnegie's company, Carnegie Steel, was producing more steel per year than all of Great Britain's steel manufacturers combined.

Stainless steel was first produced, making it possible to use steel in harsh environments where corrosion would otherwise be likely. Thanks to steel, industry as a whole became mechanized, automated, and endlessly more efficient, and mass-production technology was finally being realized.

By now, aluminum could also be produced in large enough quantities that its price declined rapidly, going from nearly twelve dollars a pound to only a few cents. It was a wonder material for manufacturers: light, malleable, resistant to corrosion, and cheap (finally!). It would become the go-to metal for consumer products like aluminum

Above: Portrait of steel tycoon, Andrew Carnegie. // Below: A meteorite from the Henbury Meteorites Conservation Reserve in Australia.

foil and cans, especially the iconic pop-tab beverage can invented in 1959.

CIRCUIT BOARDS, COMPUTERS, AND MORE

Metal also made possible developments in electronic device technology, starting with a seemingly minor innovation in 1925. An American inventor named Charles Ducas created and patented a method to easily stencil conductive metal onto a circuit board. If you ever happen to open one of your old electronics, those long, silver lines on the circuit board are actually made out of a conductive metal that sends electrical signals to various components of the device.

These circuit boards would go on to be used in the first personal computer on the market, the Programma 101 . . . and every electronic device since. The only difference today is that now, in addition

Before it was discovered that iron was readily available on earth, ancient civilizations resorted to taking iron from meteorites.

Left: Most modern office buildings and skyscrapers are built around steel girders. // Below: Terra-Cycle picture frames made from circuit boards.

to the conductive tracks, circuit boards contain metals like lead, nickel, zinc, and cadmium.

In the twenty-first century, our dependence on metals continues to grow. Some metals, such as gold and platinum, don't corrode, while others, such as steel, have the Herculean strength needed to hold up the tallest office buildings. Consumer packaging is also indebted to different kinds of metal. Your favorite brands of yogurt likely have tear-away foil lids, and most drink pouch products have a protective aluminum lining. Food and beverage containers can be made out of a variety of metals. Aluminum drink cans are the ultimate go-to for beverage convenience, and steel or tin food cans preserve our favorite perishables for months on end. Paint and aerosol cans, food trays, mint boxes, and a deluge of other types of

packaging rely on different metals to insulate, preserve, and protect the countless products we consume on a daily basis.

Our favorite smartphones, game consoles, and laptops are composed of metallic housing, gears, wires, microchips, contacts, and conductors. Some are toxic heavy metals hazardous to human health and the environment.

METALS AND OUR ENVIRONMENT

Our consumption of metal has environmental impacts beyond the material itself. When you purchase something like an aluminum soda can, for example, you subsequently drive demand for aluminum. It requires as much as 30 tons of

CAN DRUM

This music-making project repurposes two coffee cans into a set of drums, perfect for young rock stars. By combining two sizes of metal cans you can get some killer beats going that will surely bring a crowd. Remember, real rock stars always reuse, repurpose, and recycle! For ages 8 and up with adult supervision.

WHAT YOU NEED

- Cardboard
- Coffee can
- Soup can
- Old belt
- ⅛-inch-diameter rivets
- 2 tree branches
- Yarn
- Ruler
- Marker
- Scissors
- Hobby knife
- Hot glue gun
- ⅛-inch drill bit
- Drill
- Rivet gun
- Masking tape

Cut 2 (2 x 3-inch) rectangles out of your cardboard.

Using your clean and dry coffee and soup cans, trace the rounded edges of each can 1 inch apart on the rectangles you just cut.

Cut along the lines with your hobby knife.

Hot glue the cardboard shapes to the coffee cans, making sure to pair up each can to its traced edge. Press together firmly and hold until the glue has set.

5

To make the neck strap, cut the end of your belt about 6 inches from the end with the buckle, and use the hobby knife to make a very small ⅛-inch-long slit 1 inch from the cut end.

6

On the other half of the belt, make another slit 1 inch from the cut end as well.

7

Use the drill to make one ⅛-inch hole near the top of each of the coffee cans offset toward the back.

8

Push a rivet through the slit in the belt strap and into a hole previously drilled into the coffee can. Use the rivet gun to secure the belt and can together.

9

Rivet the second half of the cut belt through the hole in the opposite coffee can. Connect the two ends of the belt together.

10

To build your drumsticks, find two roughly equal-size tree branches between 10 to 14 inches long. Then, wrap yarn around an end of each stick and use masking tape to prevent the yarn from unraveling. Now you can start playing the drums!

FINISHED

aluminum ore to produce just 1 ton of aluminum. Drilling for aluminum's base ores is a resource-intensive process, often causing a significant amount of air pollution during excavation. The mines often rely on water power, and the management of dams can lead to rampant flooding. In one case in Brazil, the Tucuruí Dam caused a 600,000-acre stretch of rainforest to flood. Refining steel and mining iron carry similar environmental risks, as extremely high heat is required during smelting.

Some metals are extremely hazardous to human health and the environment, which brings us to the electronic device waste stream. About 53 million tons of electronic waste—old, discarded electronic devices—was generated in 2012. They have to go somewhere, and unfortunately that's often a third-world country where disposal is cheap. There are literally mountains of discarded electronics in countries like India, Pakistan, and China, all of which have become global dumping grounds for unwanted electronics. An old cell phone or computer monitor looks unassuming enough when all you can see is the outer casing, but metals like mercury and lead contained within can leach into the groundwater or be consumed

by wildlife after being improperly disposed of. These electronic wastelands are extremely toxic to human health, and are capable of releasing innumerable heavy metals, chemicals, and other compounds into the soil, groundwater, and air.

METAL TRASH

Any type of discarded metal material—be it e-waste, a tin can, or scrap piping from an old house—is a complete waste of a potentially long-lasting, useful material. Metal provides a level of durability in our products unmatched by most other materials, and it's in our best interest to treat it as such.

When you throw away the aluminum foil top to a yogurt tub, you are ending the lifecycle of a material that burdened the environment to produce, not to mention the permanent damage caused to the environment. What should we do with our metal trash instead?

Landfills worldwide are filling up with broken or outdated electronic equipment.

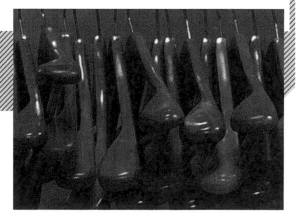

FIVE ALTERNATIVES TO COMMON HOUSEHOLD METAL PRODUCTS

Most household items made out of metal are either steel or aluminum, both of which are highly recyclable. Extracting metal from the earth is a destructive process that uses a lot of energy and releases tons of greenhouse gases into the atmosphere. Here's what you can do to lessen your contribution to the demand for these metals.

1 Banana Leaves Instead of Foil: Aluminum foil is a great way to keep food warm and toasty, but banana leaves can be an effective alternative. In fact, many people in India have been using banana leaves to wrap food in and cook with for years! Found in specialty food stores or Indian and Asian supermarkets, they are even dirt cheap.

2 Wooden Hangers: The best alternative to a wire hanger is no hanger at all, but wood hangers are okay if that's not possible. Wood is a renewable resource, and many manufacturers are certified by the Forest Stewardship Council, meaning their products are made with sustainably harvested wood.

3 Durable Cups Instead of Cans: This goes without saying: a mason jar or ceramic cup is significantly more eco-friendly than an aluminum drink can. Removing aluminum from the earth's crust is expensive, and excavation is terrible for the environment. Doesn't it sound nicer—and tastier—to drink homemade lemonade from an old jam jar than drink a six-pack of stale soda?

4 Ceramic Cookware: Iron and stainless steel are commonly used to make pots and pans because they are excellent conductors of heat. But ceramic is as well. There are many quality brands of ceramic cookware that are just as good as their metal counterparts, and they didn't have to be smelted or refined to be manufactured.

5 Wooden Flatware: Stainless steel flatware begins its long journey to your table as iron deep underground—iron that had to be mined, refined, and smelted before being mixed with additives, processed again, and turned into steel—and then designed into utensils. Wooden flatware, on the other hand, can be composted, is biodegradable (as long as it doesn't end up in a landfill), and comes from a renewable resource that is better for the environment than the production of metal items. When it's time to replace your flatware, choose greener wooden alternatives.

Above: Tamales wrapped in banana leaves ready to be steamed. // Right: A line of reusable wooden hangers.

METALS TIMELINE

4500 BCE Smelting sites for copper spring up in the Middle East, where tools like hammers are manufactured.

3500 Bronze working begins once humans realize combining molten copper with tin creates a significantly more durable material. The Bronze Age commences!

400 CE A pillar of iron is constructed in Delhi, India. It has been immortalized as the "Pillar of Delhi" as it's withstood all these years without corroding.

1810 Peter Durand patents the tin can, allowing food to be preserved for months without requiring salt or acid preservatives.

1824 Aluminum is isolated for the first time by Hans Christian Oersted. Aluminum is plentiful in the earth's crust, but is so reactive that it can only be found in compounds with other metals.

1855 Henry Bessemer patents his "Bessemer Process" for turning pig iron into steel, subsequently helping to usher in the second Industrial Revolution.

1450 While older iron objects have been discovered, the ancient Hittites from Anatolia are often credited as being the first to smelt refined iron in large quantities, mostly for weaponry.

1150 Cast iron, a strong and heavier type of iron, is forged in Europe.

1200 Iron-forging processes begin to expand across much of the West, and the Iron Age takes over.

1800 Physicist Alessandro Volta develops an early battery after discovering that metals like zinc produce a continuous electrical current when exposed to moisture.

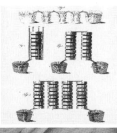

1825 William Sturgeon develops an early type of electromagnet by introducing electricity to a wire coiled around an iron bar. Today, electromagnets are found in amplifiers, toasters, and even doorbells.

1831 British scientist and inventor Michael Faraday discovers electromagnetic induction and invents the first-ever electromagnetic generator—the Faraday disk.

1862 The near-indestructible USS *New Ironsides* is commissioned by the U.S. Navy, complete with an iron-reinforced hull and 16 heavy cannons.

1875 Industrial titan and founding father of the American steel industry, Andrew Carnegie, opens his first steel mill, the Edgar Thomson Works.

1886 French scientist Paul Héroult and American inventor Charles Hall develop a method for producing commercial levels of aluminum, causing the price to plummet from twelve dollars a pound to just thirty cents.

1910 Aluminum foil can be mass-produced after a group of entrepreneurs patent a method of aluminum rolling, allowing it to be produced in a thin, long, continuous sheet.

1959 A boon to beverage companies across the world, American engineer Ermal Cleon Fraze invents an aluminum can with a pop-tab.

1890 The first skyscraper erected completely with a steel frame, the Rand McNally Building, is constructed in Chicago.

1913 English metallurgist Harry Brearley realizes that chromium increases steel's resistance to corrosion, and the first ingots of stainless steel—then called "rustless steel"—are forged.

1967 The first personal computer, the Programma 101, enters the market. With an aluminum case and sturdy metal components, the Programma 101 was as durable as it was revolutionary.

1970 Earth Day and the Environmental Protection Agency are born this year, and recycling materials like aluminum becomes more common.

2009 While steel is still recycled at higher rates than all plastics, paper, aluminum, and glass combined, over $3 billion worth of steel is still thrown away in the U.S. this year.

1900 By now, Andrew Carnegie is so successful that his company, Carnegie Steel, manufactures more steel than the entirety of Great Britain.

1925 Charles Ducas patents a way to stencil conductive metal tracks onto circuit boards. These silver tracks allow our electronics to function by transmitting signals to various components on the circuit board itself.

1989 By this year, recycling rates for aluminum drink cans increase to around 60%, more than double the rate in 1970.

2012 In the U.S., only 34% of metals that make their way into municipal solid waste are recycled. Globally, only about one-third of all metals have above a 50% recovery rate.

1908 Ford's Model T car, made out of strong and lightweight vanadium steel, enters the consumer market.

TODAY Metals have undoubtedly accelerated the progress of civilization: electrical wiring, cars, drink cans, airplanes, and the list goes on. While some of these metals are highly recyclable, the heavy-metal-containing e-waste we're generating at an exponential rate is not.

FORK PLACE-CARD HOLDER

Thrift shops and yard sales often have old, mismatched flatware. Pick up a few forks to create some unique, individualized photo displays or place-card holders. Some metals bend easier than others, so grab a few spares. For ages 16 and up.

WHAT YOU NEED

/ Silver fork
/ Two pieces of heavy fabric or leather scraps
/ Vise
/ Lighter
/ Propane torch
/ Pliers
/ Glass of water
/ Leather gloves (optional)

Wrap the pronged end of the fork with a piece of the heavyweight fabric or leather, and place in the vise grip, with the front of the fork facing toward you. The fabric protects the fork from scratches. Clamp tightly.

Light the propane torch, keeping the flame small. Heat the fork at the neck, just above the clamp. Be sure the fabric doesn't catch fire; keep a glass of water nearby in case. Hold the torch to the fork for about 30 seconds. Turn off the flame.

Wrap the neck of the fork with the heavy fabric, just above the heated area, and use the pliers to bend the neck down and away from you.

If the neck is still hot enough, pull it to the left at about a 45-degree angle. If the neck is not bending easily, you may need to apply more heat.

Next, while holding the hot fork with pliers, remove from the vise and plunge into water to cool.

6 Wrap the rounded tip of the fork in fabric, about 2 inches from the end, and place in the vise grip with the front facing you. Clamp tightly. Light the torch again, and heat the area just above where the fork is in the vise. Watch that the flame does not come in contact with the fabric.

7 Wrap the center area of the fork stem with fabric, and grip with pliers and twist the fork to the left and down again.

8 Remove from vise using pliers and plunge in water to cool. Place a place card or photo in the tines of the fork and enjoy!

METALS TODAY

Most metals are highly recyclable — all it takes is for them to be melted once again and reforged. Steel, for instance, was recycled at a rate of 88 percent in 2012 in the U.S. Steel can be recycled endlessly as well, preserving 100 percent of its original strength each time it is reprocessed. There is a demand for steel, iron, and other hard metal scrap, so these materials enjoy a high recycling rate.

Around the world, about 76 percent of postconsumer aluminum beverage cans are recycled every year. Aluminum cans collected for recycling are also quickly turned around, becoming new aluminum products in a matter of months after entering into your recycling bin.

HARD METALS

Steel, iron, and titanium are just a few types of hard metals. They are typically rigid and inflexible, strong, often heavy, and can be fairly brittle. These are the metals that maintain our infrastructure, support multistory buildings, and make the machines and assembly lines that facilitate our manufacturing and production needs.

Steel is one of the most important hard metals, but producing it can be a blight on the environment. To make steel, large amounts of iron need to be mined and collected. Mining and excavation require significant amounts of energy, and create an array of environmental problems. For one, mining deep into the earth can expose radioactive materials that have been buried under hard rock for millions of years. Once they are uncovered, they can release dangerous chemicals, elements, and compounds into the air and surrounding groundwater. Dust

TIP: EXPERIMENT WITH A FEW FORKS FIRST TO GET THE ANGLES AND BALANCE CORRECT.

The finest workers in stone are not copper or steel tools, but the gentle touches of air and water working at their leisure with a liberal allowance of time.
—HENRY DAVID THOREAU

According to the U.S. Geological Survey, the average American will use approximately 1,300 pounds of copper, in some form or another, throughout his or her entire life.

FIVE METAL OBJECTS YOU AREN'T RECYCLING (BUT TOTALLY COULD BE)

So you recycle aluminum cans like there is no tomorrow. That's great! But there are countless other metal products that you probably didn't even realize can be recycled. Some, you can even make money recycling.

1 **Everything Steel:** The market for steel is so huge that just about anything made out of it can be recycled. So before you throw away your old toaster, food cans, or even an unused pet cage, do a quick search in your area to find scrap recyclers near you.

2 **Bottle Caps:** Metal bottle caps are typically made out of aluminum or steel, both of which are highly recyclable. The problem is the caps are so small that most people don't even think to save them or place them in the recycling bin. Even if they have a thin layer of plastic on the underside they can still be recycled; the plastic will evaporate when the metal is heated.

3 **Batteries:** Whether it's the lithium ion battery in your smartphone or the alkaline battery in your remote control, most batteries can be recycled. Most phone manufacturers and service providers offer lithium ion battery recycling, just like most car dealerships accept old car batteries. Many municipal programs accept everyday alkaline batteries, too.

4 **Cookware:** Chances are that most of your pots, pans, baking sheets, skillets, and other cookware are made out of some type of metal. If your old cookware is still in decent condition, consider donating it to a secondhand store like Goodwill for reuse. If that isn't an option, there are many scrap metal recyclers that are willing to accept a wide variety of metal products. Be sure to check online before bringing them your cookware, as some only accept ferrous metals (like iron and steel), while others only accept nonferrous metals (like aluminum and copper).

5 **Wire Hangers:** These can be made out of a small variety of metals, but it's often hard to identify which kind just by looking at them. Many curbside programs will actually accept wire hangers included in the recycling bin, but investigate yourself to see if this is the case. Otherwise, simply stop at the dry cleaners—most will accept any hangers at no cost.

Opposite: Metal factory.
// Above: Various beverage bottle caps. // Left: Batteries are mostly made of metal and can be recycled in many places.

MINT TIN SURVIVAL KIT

Mint tins are a great reusable container for life's necessities. With this DIY you are sure to have all of the items you need in case of an emergency situation in the palm of your hand. Make a few and leave them in various places like your backpack or car so you are always prepared. For ages 12 and up.

WHAT YOU NEED

/ Mint tin
/ 180 or 320 grit sandpaper
/ Metal polish
/ Orange spray paint
/ Electrical tape
/ Super glue
/ Mini compass
/ Matchbook

1
Start with a clean and empty mint tin. Use the sandpaper to remove the paint on the bottom of the tin. Start with the roughest grit, and finish on the finest.

2
Use the metal polish to further shine up the bottom. You want to achieve a mirrorlike finish, which can be used to signal aircraft for help or inspect injuries.

3
Use the orange spray paint on all sides except the bottom. Make sure to paint it while closed, as to not get paint inside the container.

4
Seal the opening by adhering electrical tape between the top and bottom of the tin. Add more tape near the hinges to prevent water from leaking in.

5
Super glue the mini compass to the top of the tin.

TIP: MAKE SURE YOU SPRAY PAINT IN AN AREA WITH GOOD VENTILATION.

Super glue the matchbook to the inside of the tin, either on the left or right side.

Now that the basics of survival are covered, feel free to add additional items to your kit. Potential additions could include: antibiotic ointment, aspirin, bandages, water purification tablets, utility knife blades, safety pins, 2 feet of aluminum foil, a few yards of nylon string, wire, needle and thread, rubber bands, $20, birthday candle, pencil, whistle, and tweezers. Place your kit in your everyday bag or with your camping gear, in case you ever need it!

particulates, some similar to asbestos, are also released into the air.

Once hard metals like iron are mined, they then enter the smelting process. Smelting is another energy-intensive process, and burning coal is often required to achieve the high energy levels that are needed. Aside from the obvious damage from coal burning, compounds like iron oxide, fluorides, and certain heavy metals are released into the air when producing metals like steel. While there are precautions and standards in place to control carbon and other pollutant emissions, there are many places along the production line where leaks and compromises can occur.

Needless to say, carbon emissions throughout the process are incredibly high. Based on calculations by the Environmental Protection Agency and the Department of Energy, the U.S. iron and steel industry is responsible for generating as much as 224 million metric tons of carbon dioxide per year, one of the primary contributors to global warming and climate change.

SOFT METALS

These metals are often lightweight, resistant to corrosion, and malleable enough to be bent considerably without breaking. They make for excellent packaging, as they maintain the integrity of a product without adding too much bulk or weight. A soft metal such as aluminum is able to take the form of foil wrap, a protective lining (on individual apple sauce and yogurts, for example), or even a rigid drink can.

As mentioned previously, aluminum is highly recyclable and there is a large market for the recycled material, but we need to look beyond the material itself. Extracting aluminum from the ground uses an outrageous amount of energy. Aluminum, as we know it, isn't found freely in the earth's crust—an aluminum-containing ore called bauxite is extracted from the ground and processed into aluminum. Coal burning is required

In contrast [to trees and fish], oil, metals, and coal are not renewable; they don't reproduce, sprout, or have sex to produce baby oil droplets or coal nuggets.

— JARED DIAMOND, *Collapse: How Societies Choose to Fail or Succeed*

during the aluminum-smelting process, which also sends perfluorocarbons into the air. Perfluorocarbons are more than 9,000 times more dangerous than carbon dioxide, as far as global warming and climate change are concerned.

ELECTRONIC WASTE

Fifty-three million tons of electronics were trashed in 2012, and it's a safe bet that this number will increase in the future. The need for instant gratification, be it for communication or entertainment, has led to a massive spike in the number of electronic devices on the market. For some perspective, research by the computer network hardware company Cisco states that there will be more cell phones than people on earth by the end of 2014. By 2018, the average will increase further to 1.4 devices per person!

That's a lot of devices, and quite a lot of obsolete electronic waste that will be generated between now and then. This e-waste can contain a toxic cocktail of various metal components that can have long-lasting health and environmental risks if left unmanaged for long, which is presently the case in many countries where e-waste is dumped, such as China, Ghana, Nigeria, India, Bangladesh, and Pakistan. Certain metals like cadmium, lead, and chromium can accumulate in people and wildlife through contaminated food, water, and direct contact with the materials when left in e-waste graveyards. People living near e-waste can be exposed to other chemicals such as polychlorinated biphenyls (what refrigerators once contained as a primary coolant), either through inhalation or ingestion via contaminated food or

Trucks loaded with metal
ore leave a strip mine.

These cubes are made of crushed aluminum cans ready to be recycled.

Two hundred billion canned-food products are made every year.

water. Today, polychlorinated biphenyls can be found in oil-based paint, adhesives, and tape, and many plastics, but efforts to discontinue its use are ongoing. E-waste also commonly contains precious metals like gold, silver, and palladium, enticing scrap-seekers and e-waste landfill scavengers to expose themselves to these hazardous areas in an effort to collect the valuable materials.

One of the primary concerns with e-waste is that there is no simple recycling method. Because materials like printed circuit boards contain so many microcomponent parts and hazardous heavy metals, separation and processing can be especially tricky to manage—and it's expensive. This is why as much as 80 percent of the e-waste that is collected is simply sent to developing countries

instead of being properly reprocessed or recycled.

How much e-waste actually exists? At the current rate of production, twenty years from now there will be over 1 billion tons of e-waste scattered around the planet. To make matters worse, e-waste is expected to grow at a rate of 8 percent every year. And most of it is simply thrown in a landfill.

LOOKING FORWARD

Since the first miraculous ores of metal were mined thousands of years ago, humans have, where possible, adapted it into every facet of life. When industry prevailed and began to modernize every

Left: Broken electronics reveal the many different types of materials used to make them. // Below: Aluminum ingots ready to be processed into a product.

corner of human existence, metals of all shapes, sizes, and varieties played a key role. It's as prevalent as plastic, but attracts far less attention from environmentalists because of its recyclablity. But excavating and mining for aluminum ore is a huge environmental stressor.

At TerraCycle we rarely work with products or packages that are purely metal, as those tend to be recycled the most (like a can of soda). Instead we find metal in all forms of products and packages, mixed together with plastics and other material types. From a coffee capsule, which is partly metal and partly plastic, to a pen, which is part plastic, part rubber, and part metal, to even a drink pouch, which is a layer of flexible plastic combined with a layer of flexible metal.

In each of these cases we focus first on creating national collection platforms where you can collect these waste streams for free and have

them sent to TerraCycle to be recycled. These waste streams need to be collected separately as the process to recycle them is different for each one.

A coffee capsule, for example, has to be shredded so that we can separate the coffee and other organics (like tea and milk) from the plastic and aluminum. The organics are then composted, and the plastic and aluminum are further separated. Once complete the aluminum is melted and sold to various companies that can use it to make their products (reducing the need for new aluminum to be extracted); the same occurs for the plastic once it is melted and refined.

Writing instruments undergo a similar process with separation focusing on plastics versus rubbers versus metals. The trick is first separating out the component materials, which still to this day happens manually.

LIFECYCLE OF AN ALUMINUM CAN

An aluminum can starts as an unrefined mineral, known as bauxite ore, located in the earth's crust. The ore is mined in large quantities and shipped for processing.

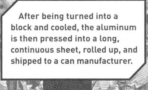

After being turned into a block and cooled, the aluminum is then pressed into a long, continuous sheet, rolled up, and shipped to a can manufacturer.

Huge rolls of aluminum are needed at the aluminum can manufacturing facility. Some rolls weigh as much as twelve tons, measuring almost six miles long. These massive spools are unrolled with a machine called an uncoiler, which then lubricates the metal and sends the flattened sheet through the beverage can assembly line.

First up is shaping the can. This starts with a machine called a cupping press, which will cut the sheet of aluminum into small discs and form them into rounded cup shapes — nearly 4,000 cups can be made every minute!

The newly cut cans are then formed into taller, longer cylinders that more closely resemble the iconic aluminum cans we all know. After a cutting machine ensures they are all the same size, the cans are washed.

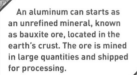

After acquiring the ore, it can then be refined into an aluminum and oxygen compound called aluminum oxide. A current of electricity then breaks down the aluminum oxide, melting the aluminum into a molten pool of hot metal. The isolated aluminum is then combined with other additives and metals to strengthen it and make it more resilient.

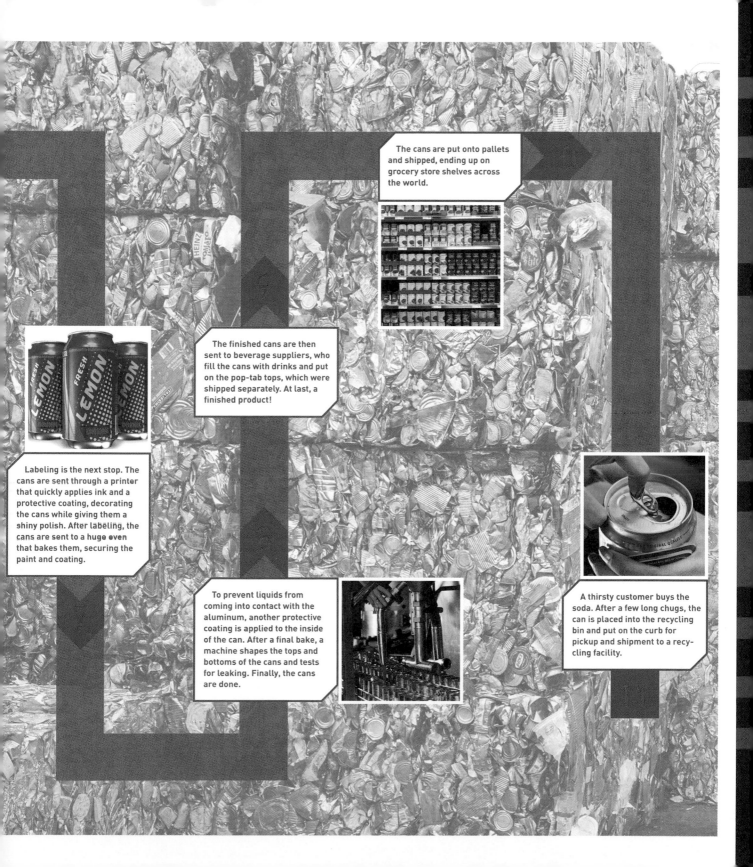

The cans are put onto pallets and shipped, ending up on grocery store shelves across the world.

The finished cans are then sent to beverage suppliers, who fill the cans with drinks and put on the pop-tab tops, which were shipped separately. At last, a finished product!

Labeling is the next stop. The cans are sent through a printer that quickly applies ink and a protective coating, decorating the cans while giving them a shiny polish. After labeling, the cans are sent to a huge oven that bakes them, securing the paint and coating.

To prevent liquids from coming into contact with the aluminum, another protective coating is applied to the inside of the can. After a final bake, a machine shapes the tops and bottoms of the cans and tests for leaking. Finally, the cans are done.

A thirsty customer buys the soda. After a few long chugs, the can is placed into the recycling bin and put on the curb for pickup and shipment to a recycling facility.

And with a juice pouch, TerraCycle's solution was to make an aluminumized plastic compound that can be used to make plastic benches and other outdoor furniture. A small percentage of the pouches are upcycled, by sewing individual pouches together to make countless consumer products, from tote bags to wallets and backpacks. The packaging's multicomponent properties, once a huge obstacle to recyclability, could finally be worked around in a sustainable way.

Even e-waste has a solution. Companies like TerraCycle, and many others, offer free and paid e-waste collection programs. Typically the free programs are for high-value electronics that can be refurbished and resold to consumers who can't afford new electronic products. The paid ones are typically for e-waste that doesn't have such secondary markets and has to be shredded and recycled.

As with all waste streams the solution isn't only proper recycling, it's buying smarter. If you buy products made from metals, try to buy ones that don't combine other material types together, such as plastics, papers, or organics, as that will make it very hard to recycle in a traditional way.

Right: TerraCycle makes a line of upcycled products, like this clock, from used circuit boards. // Far right: A child sits on a pile of e-waste. // Opposite: A power plant.

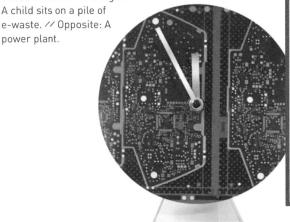

The e-Stewards Initiative

FOR MANY MANUFACTURERS and recyclers, it's simply easier and cheaper to ship electronic waste overseas to willing takers than it is to find a safer alternative.

This is where the e-Stewards Initiative comes in. Initiated by the Basel Action Network, a Seattle-based nonprofit focused on stopping the trade of toxic materials to developing countries, the e-Stewards Initiative is an attempt to prevent toxic electronic scrap from being improperly disposed of, or from being shipped overseas.

The e-Stewards Certification program is the primary line of defense, bringing desperately needed social responsibility to a waste stream that has quickly grown out of control. Companies that recycle electronic waste can become "e-Stewards Certified" following a series of audits, while meeting strict processing guidelines. For instance, certified recyclers are prohibited from incinerating waste containing arsenic, mercury, or beryllium. Hazardous waste, or waste that meets certain toxin benchmarks, must be disposed of at hazardous-waste disposal facilities. Facilities that recyclers send waste to must also meet specific emission capture-rate guidelines.

Dozens of companies, dubbed "e-Stewards Enterprises," have partnered with the organization's certified recyclers to ensure their electronic waste is responsibly processed. Bank of America, Boeing, LG Electronics, and Staples are just a few, and more are likely to join in the coming years.

Like Fair Trade Coffee and other social responsibility certification programs, the e-Stewards Initiative brings accountability and transparency to industries that deal with this poisonous waste stream.

And Man created the plastic bag and the tin and aluminum can and the cellophane wrapper and the paper plate, and this was good because Man could then take his automobile and buy all his food in one place and He could save that which was good to eat in the refrigerator and throw away that which had no further use. And soon the earth was covered with plastic bags and aluminum cans and paper plates and disposable bottles and there was nowhere to sit down or walk, and Man shook his head and cried: "Look at this Godawful mess."

—ART BUCHWALD

More than three cubic yards of space, about the size of a Dumpster, are saved in landfills for every ton of paper that is recycled.

CHAPTER 3

PAPER

Long before the age of digital recording and the Internet, human beings resorted to the spoken word or writing by hand to record their thoughts, stories, and ideas. Paper and its early counterparts, papyrus and parchment, allowed knowledge to transcend time, passing information on from civilization to civilization. 　　While today paper used for spreading information is slowly being usurped by the digital media of the Information Age, its usefulness as a material hasn't shrunk—quite the opposite. Every year nearly 400 million tons of paper is used up globally.

Whether for food packaging, cardboard shipping boxes, pizza boxes, disposable cups and plates, even newspapers and magazines, paper has evolved into a wonder material due to its low cost and the seemingly endless supply of trees to cut down.

NON-WOOD PAPERS

Surprisingly, the wood-based paper dominating the world today is a relatively recent invention. Before our shift to wood, early civilizations instead used plants, parchment made from dried livestock skin, and tablets made of rock or clay.

The papyrus plant was used as an early form of paper, especially by the Egyptians around 3000 BCE. Papyrus was plentiful around the Nile, and the process of turning it into paper was relatively simple. Still, the plant was really only available around the Nile Delta, limiting its usefulness outside the area.

Across the continent in China, a breakthrough in papermaking came in 105 CE when a member of the Imperial Court named Ts'ai Lun presented to the emperor the first documented method for making paper. Ts'ai Lun's paper was made with a

mix of plant material, such as mulberry bark, and shredded rags, which were then mashed into a pulp, pressed into molds, and dried into sheets. Instead of having to rely on a single plant like papyrus, this technique meant that a variety of different fibrous plants and rags could be used for pulp.

Papermaking eventually found its way into Korea around 500, where bamboo, mulberry, hemp, and other plants were used as the pulp base. Similar techniques eventually left Korea for Japan in 610, after a Korean Buddhist monk shared his knowledge of papermaking with Japan's emperor. Even though the process was spreading throughout the East, it still required a skilled papermaker with knowledge of Chinese techniques in order to be successful.

SPREADING THE PAPERMAKING SECRET

In 751, a battle between Chinese and Arab forces changed this. After confronting one another at the Talas River in Central Asia, Arab forces viciously defeated the Chinese army in one of the most important victories in human history. What makes the Battle of Talas so noteworthy is that captured Chinese prisoners of war also happened to be skilled papermakers. After being taken back to the city of Samarkand in present-day Uzbekistan, the prisoners of war were forced to share their knowledge, and papermaking began to spread throughout the Middle East. The secret was finally out.

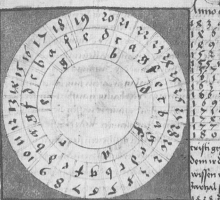

Left: An exhibit from the Robert C. Williams Paper Museum in Atlanta, Georgia, illustrating the papermaking process. // Center: A variety of newspapers from around the world. // Bottom: The Fourdrinier machine was one of the first ways to mass-produce paper.

Of the 104 billion individual pieces of junk mail sent to Americans every single year, 44% of them will get to a landfill without ever even being opened.

No longer a mystery to the world, papermaking could finally be developed across the globe. One of the most important developments came about when linen, a textile made from the flax plant, was introduced to the pulping process. Textiles like linen and cotton cloth are fantastic additions to pulp, as their fibers are durable and can last for years. Cotton and linen rags would even go on to be one of the common primary ingredients in paper pulp all around the world for thousands of years.

It took some time, but the paper revolution officially reached the West in 1276 when a paper mill was built in Italy—the first of its kind in all of Europe. With a burgeoning paper industry, paper products like books, manuscripts, novels, and official documents could be manufactured far quicker than before. Even so, copying an existing book or document still required text to be meticulously copied by hand, letter by letter. That would all change in 1448 thanks to German printer Johann Gutenberg and his invention of movable type.

By forging individual letters out of metal, words could be systematically arranged on the printing press to make words and sentences. This meant that entire documents could be copied in a fraction of the time required by normal handwritten copying, and the cost of paper products like books and newspapers fell as a result. Knowledge and written information could finally be mass-produced!

FROM RAGS TO TREES

Soon after the first paper mill in America was built in 1690, the world found itself faced with an exciting new Industrial Revolution. Widespread innovations and new technologies began to seep into every aspect of industry, including the world

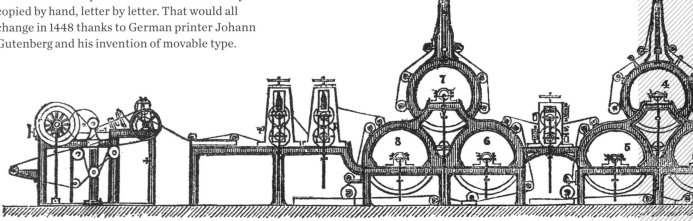

Left: Stacks of newspapers outside a newsstand. //
Right: Portrait of Friedrich Keller.

of papermaking. For instance, the Fourdrinier papermaking machine, developed at the end of the eighteenth century, made it possible to produce 1,000 pounds of paper a day instead of only 100.

Techniques for de-inking paper were developed at this time as well, finally making it possible to recycle paper with text or print. Chlorine bleach was used more frequently to whiten paper pulp. In 1817, the cardboard box was invented.

But even with all of this innovation, there was still a raw material problem. Papermakers up to now had largely used textile rags to make the pulp mash necessary to manufacture paper. But by the early eighteenth century, people began to realize that the supply of rags was being stretched thin, so much so that intellectuals and inventors suggested replacing rags with materials like hemp, even asbestos! Rags were so widely used in countries like the U.S. that they even began to be imported

from parts of Europe, and the global supply of rags fell significantly. It was clear that a true replacement was desperately needed, and fast.

German inventor Friedrich Keller revolutionized the paper industry in the nineteenth century by focusing on a single, simple material: wood. He invented a machine that was able to grind and mash wood into a pulp, and a massive new market was immediately opened for this lucrative, and especially abundant, raw material. No longer would papermakers have to struggle to accumulate rags. Finding the necessary raw materials was as simple as looking to the trees in the forest.

Needless to say, wood was quick to catch on. By 1870, the *New York Times* was being printed solely on wood-based paper, becoming the first newspaper to fully adopt the new kind of paper. Only a few years later, another German inventor named Carl F. Dahl patented the "kraft process," a way to break wood down into pulp with chemicals instead of machinery. Papermakers also began to use compounds like barium sulfate to give paper a shiny gloss, like we see on the pages of present-day magazines.

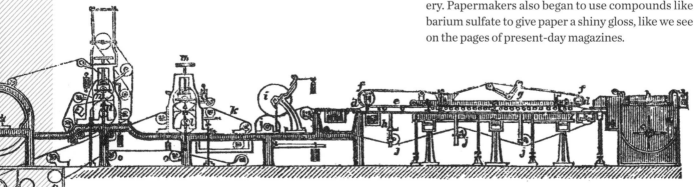

PAPER TIMELINE

1684 In an attempt to find a replacement for linen and cotton rags, British publisher Edward Lloyd suggests in the journal *Philosophical Transactions* that paper could be made from asbestos.

751 Arab and Chinese forces fight at the Battle of Talas in Central Asia. After a decisive victory, Arabian forces learn that their Chinese prisoners are skilled papermakers. The secrets of Chinese papermaking are revealed.

3000 BCE Papyrus and livestock-skin parchment are among the first forms of paper used in recorded history.

806 China begins to use paper currency, making so much of it throughout the next several hundred years that inflation eventually skyrockets.

1276 The first paper mill in Europe appears in the town of Fabriano, Italy. Manuscripts, books, and documents galore are written. The growing paper industry makes the written word available to everyone.

1690 Papermaker and entrepreneur William Rittenhouse builds the first paper mill on American soil in Germantown, Pennsylvania. The mill even began replacing virgin materials with recycled rags.

105 CE Papermaking techniques are introduced to the Chinese Emperor by Ts'ai Lun, a member of the Imperial Court, marking the first record of an official papermaking process.

1031 The first known practice of recycling paper occurs in Japan, where papermakers turn old, trashed paper into pulp for new batches.

1448 Johann Gutenberg perfects his "movable type" invention for the printing press. With individual letters cast out of metal, it became possible to easily mass-produce books, newspapers, and documents.

1716 In an essay published in London, "The Society of Gentlemen" describes how hemp, after being dried and pressed, could be used as an alternative to linen and rags, the supply of which was unstable.

500 The first instances of papermaking in Korea pop up; the pulp mash consisted of plant materials like bamboo, mulberry, and hemp.

610 A Buddhist monk from Korea enlightens Japan's emperor with his papermaking knowledge. As Buddhism continues to spread across Asia, so too does the practice of papermaking.

1804 Chlorine bleaching agents are used for the first time in a U.S. paper mill.

1890 Barium sulfate is used more frequently to give paper the glossy sheen noticeable in magazines.

1980 In the 1970s, mills could make more than 250 tons of recycled paper a day. As technology improved throughout the 1980s, that number increased to as high as 1,000 tons, overtaking the virgin paper market.

1817 Cardboard boxes for commercial use are created in England for the first time.

1897 The first recycling center in the U.S. opens in New York City; it recycles metals, burlap, carpeting, and paper.

1993 For the first time in the U.S., more paper ends up recycled than landfilled. President Bill Clinton even begins requiring government agencies to buy paper containing at least 20% recycled material.

2012 As of this year, Americans alone are generating about 30 million tons of paper waste annually.

1848 Friedrich Keller makes it possible to mass-produce wood paper by inventing the wood-grinding pulping machine.

1900 The utility and cost-effectiveness of cardboard is realized, as paperboard and stiff paper boxes start to replace handmade, commercial wooden shipping containers.

1995 By now, there are over 400 different types of recycled paper available on the market.

TODAY In the U.S., paper comprises about 27% of all landfill waste generated each year. Every single day around the world, about 1 million tons of paper is used and the average per capita consumption globally is about 120 pounds a year. Without comprehensive, global reforestation efforts, cutting down billions of trees every single year is not sustainable.

1879 Carl F. Dahl invents the "kraft process," a technique for making pulp by digesting wood with chemicals instead of pulping mechanically.

1916 World War I supply shortages abound, and the U.S. government urges people to donate their old rags and paper for recycling.

2007 A report by the United Nations roughly estimates that anywhere from 3 to 6 billion trees are cut down every year. Forty-three percent of those trees are used to make paper or paper products.

1970 As plastics become an industry preference, paper and cardboard are used less frequently for product packaging.

2010 By now, humans around the world consume 400 million tons of paper each year.

The tree which moves some to tears of joy is in the eyes of others only a green thing that stands in the way. Some see nature all ridicule and deformity . . . and some scarce see nature at all. But to the eyes of the man of imagination, nature is imagination itself.

— WILLIAM BLAKE

504
POUNDS

Human beings consume an average of 120 pounds of paper products per person every year. In North America and Europe, the average is even higher at 504 and 393 pounds, respectively.

PAPER RECYCLING

A few decades after Keller changed the face of the paper industry forever, the U.S. established its first recycling center, based in New York City. The center opened in 1897, marking the first time that metals, textiles, and paper could be collected, sorted, and recycled on a municipal level. What makes this particularly special for paper is that it is extremely recyclable, capable of replacing virgin materials in the manufacturing process many times over. Paper's recyclability was fully realized with the onset of World War I, as supply shortages forced the government into begging the public for old books and other paper products. Recycling wasn't just a fad; it was absolutely necessary.

Since then, the market for recycled paper has exploded—making it is often cheaper than producing virgin paper. By the 1980s paper mills were so efficient they could make thousands of tons of recycled paper a day.

In 1993, for the first time ever, more paper was recycled than trashed in landfills, and it was the same year that President Bill Clinton passed a bill requiring government agencies to only buy paper made with some recycled material. One would think this indicates we are fast-approaching a more sustainable future, but that's not entirely the case.

We still consume hundreds of millions of tons of paper each year, most of it coming from wood.

And we cut down a lot of trees to make that happen. It's estimated that 3 billion trees are cut down every year worldwide—some research suggests that number may be as high as 6 billion—to sustain the global demand for wood- and paper-based products. That includes anything and everything from cardboard to copier paper, toilet paper, and packaging. To date, we have collectively and systematically removed nearly half of all the forest area on earth!

That unassuming piece of copier paper really isn't eco-friendly after all.

By observing wasps, French scientist René de Réaumur realized that paper might be able to be produced with wood. The wasps would take wood fibers and use them to make paper-like materials to construct their nests.

Opposite: Paper milling uses large amounts of water and can destroy nearby rivers. // Above: Magazines on a store shelf.

About 80,000 trees would need to be planted daily to offset the amount of paper towels thrown away every day.

Right: Newspapers on a modern high-speed printing press. // Opposite: Garbage piled high in a landfill.

PAPER TODAY

Not all paper products are created equal. Many types of paper packaging that have had direct contact with food, especially oily and greasy food, cannot be recycled. The grease and food residue that remains on the packaging can contaminate other recyclables when undergoing processing. Any type of wax-coated cardboard or paper boxes, like those used for many types of produce, are likewise not recyclable.

Other types of paper have less noticeable, seemingly benign differences in their composition that can make them unrecyclable or dangerous to the environment. Paper that has been bleached with chlorine may not be accepted for recycling, as it risks leaching chlorine into the earth and groundwater. Coated glossy paper, like that used for photographs, is not always recyclable either.

The good news: Americans recycled 65 percent of the paper waste they generated in 2012. Newspapers and magazines are generally accepted at most municipal recycling centers, and a large number of paper products have begun to use or increase the use of recycled paper in the manufacturing process. In the U.S., around 80 percent of paper mills have the infrastructure in place to use municipally recycled paper during production.

THE GREAT DEBATE: PAPER OR PLASTIC?

The debate between paper grocery bags and plastic grocery bags has been ongoing for years. Which is a more eco-friendly product? Plastic doesn't biodegrade and it comes from unsustainable petroleum, so paper might seem like the better option. Not necessarily. For one, paper bag production can cause as much as 70 percent more air pollution than plastic bag production. To confound things further, more paper is required to make a bag that's as strong as a plastic bag, meaning more materials are required, more water is consumed, and more energy is used.

But the paper bag is biodegradable, right? Not always. If any paper product gets sent to a landfill, it will be buried deep underneath a massive mound of garbage. No access to sunlight or oxygen inevitably means that biodegradation can't happen, thus the paper remains there in the landfill indefinitely. Landfills are truly horrible for the environment, too, as their only real contributions are providing places for us to be in denial about our trash; landfills release massive amounts of methane into the atmosphere (which is more than 20 times as potent as carbon dioxide). This debate has so many influencing factors that it's hard to say for sure which material, paper or plastic, is truly more eco-friendly. As a better alternative, use reusable tote bags made out of 100 percent recycled textile or post-consumer plastic. You'll be limiting the usage of virgin materials, won't be feeding demand for raw wood or plastic, and can reuse the bags over and over again.

IMPACT ON THE ENVIRONMENT

From a manufacturing point of view, making paper isn't exactly an eco-friendly process. For one, it requires a lot of water: three gallons of water, up and down the manufacturing process, to produce one sheet of paper. That seems like a lot, but it's even more alarming when you consider that only 2.5 percent of the water on earth is fresh water, and clean fresh water can be even harder to find in third-world and developing countries.

The billions of trees that are chopped down every year is a staggering number; about 40 percent of these are used to make paper products.

Even though paper is often biodegradable, being buried in a landfill with no access to oxygen or sunlight often means it won't quickly biodegrade.

Wood-derived paper isn't necessarily the whole problem, it's the fact that the entire system

> I think, on a personal level, everybody, when you go through the checkout line after you get your groceries and they say, "Paper or plastic?" We should be saying, "Neither one." We should have our own cloth bags.
>
> — WOODY HARRELSON

FOOD BOX POETRY MAGNETS

Turn your food boxes and refrigerator magnets into art that talks! Gather a few refrigerator magnets and an old food box to make some magnetic words and keep them both out of the landfill. The random combinations of words can be gut-bustingly hilarious. Use them in your home or office carefully. Too much hilarity has been linked to a rise in laughter and smiles. For ages 6 and up with adult supervision.

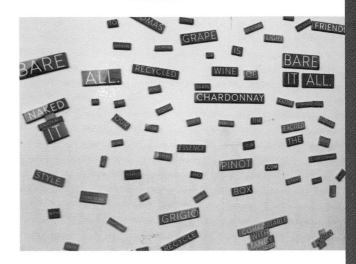

WHAT YOU NEED

- Food box
- Hobby knife and cutting mat, or scissors
- Contact cement
- Rubber refrigerator magnets
- Ruler
- Pencil

0

1

Open up your food box and use a hobby knife or scissors to cut out the panels you would like to use. Make sure to use panels with lots of words and fun elements you would like as a magnet.

2

Apply contact cement to the back of the box panel and the fridge magnets individually. Wait for both to get tacky, and carefully press together. Press tightly for a few minutes to adhere.

Unlike glass and many metals, paper can be recycled only so many times. This is because the recycling process shortens the cellulose fibers every time, degrading its suitability for papermaking.

3

Use your ruler to mark straight lines. Use a hobby knife or scissors to cut out the individual words or elements. Stick them on your fridge.

Crumpled sticky notes.

FIVE WAYS YOUR FAMILY CAN USE LESS PAPER

Whether writing a list of groceries, printing a homework assignment, drying your hands in the kitchen, or even just thumbing through your favorite magazine, you are using paper all day long. Try to lessen your household's dependence on paper products by following a few of these tips.

1 Get Techy: Could laptops and tablets be the answer to wasted classroom paper? Industry analysts expect schools in the U.S. to purchase 3.5 million tablets by the end of 2014. From grades K to 12, teachers are implementing technology: sending video lessons on snow days and replacing arithmetic sheets with math apps, not only expanding educational opportunities, but saving crumpled-up handouts from the bottom of backpacks nationwide. Electronic devices come with their own package of environmental issues, but as long as they are not replaced frequently and discarded irresponsibly, they can be excellent eco-alternatives.

2 Ban the Brown Bag: It's time to bring back the old-school lunchbox. Sending a child with a brown-bag lunch generates an average of 65 pounds of garbage each year per child. One-third of that waste is from paper alone, which means switching to reusable lunch carriers and cloth napkins can save a whole lot of trash.

3 Two Sides Are Better Than One: By adopting a double-sided policy at home, school, and work, paper waste is cut in half. Set printer defaults to double-sided and use one-sided documents as scrap paper.

4 Un-stick from Sticky Notes: They're no longer fun and cute in a landfill. An estimated 80 billion notes are used each year, and not all recycling mills can process the adhesive that makes them sticky. Attaching dry-erase boards to a cubical wall or keeping one on an office desk is a great way to de-clutter and keep those notes from the trash.

5 Opt for E-bills: Switching to online billing can save time, money, and trees. By avoiding paper statements, bills, and payments, Americans could save more than 9 million trees per year. Most credit card, utility, phone service, and cable companies actually prefer online correspondence.

involved in making that cardboard box or magazine is unsustainable. The paper industry today is one of the biggest contributors to greenhouse gas emissions, releasing more dangerous toxins into the environment with every new sheet of paper produced. The hazardous chemicals often used to digest wood into pulp can also find their way into natural bodies of water, as paper and pulp facilities are often located near a water supply.

/ LOOKING FORWARD /

At TerraCycle we have tried to look at how we can help recycle hard-to-recycle paper waste and how we can make paper from other materials beyond wood fiber. Hard-to-recycle paper waste is all around us, from our coffee cups (which are hard

LIFECYCLE OF A MAGAZINE

The black liquor can be turned back into cooking chemicals, or burned at the mill for energy.

To make pulp, the bark must first be removed.

After cooking, the result-ing pulp is brown. To make it white, it must be bleached with chlorine or more eco-friendly chlorine-free bleach. Additives to change brightness, opacity, and other traits of the paper are also combined with the pulp.

After cooking, the remaining chemicals and wood byproducts are washed away from the pre-cious wood pulp. The leftover materials and chemicals from the cooking process are known as black liquor.

The logs are then chipped and heated, also called cooking, in a pressurized chemical bath.

To make coated paper, it's important that the pulping chemicals dissolve all the wood's lignin, or what binds the wood fibers together.

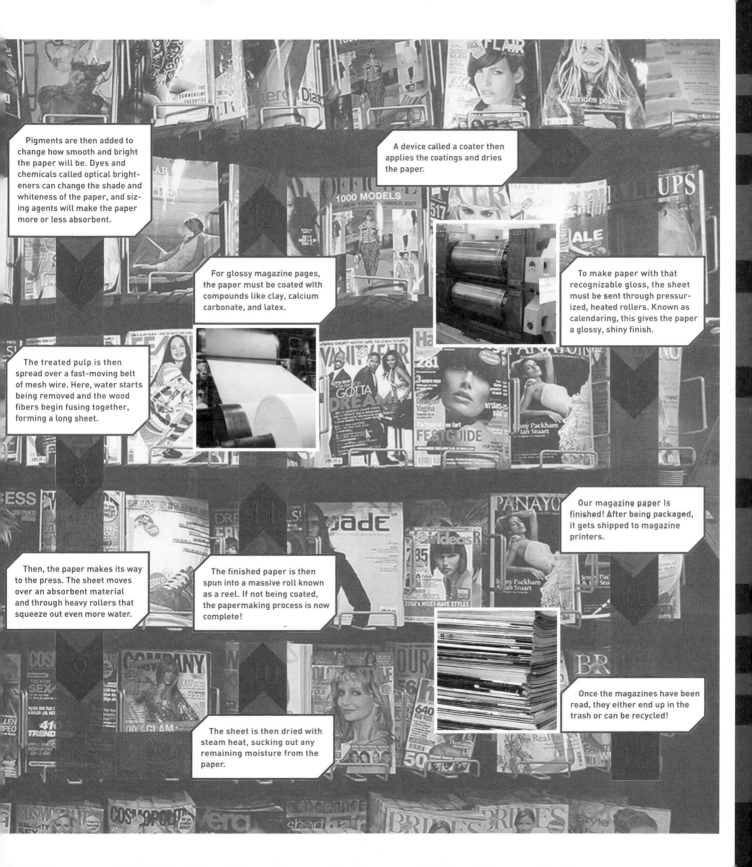

Pigments are then added to change how smooth and bright the paper will be. Dyes and chemicals called optical brighteners can change the shade and whiteness of the paper, and sizing agents will make the paper more or less absorbent.

A device called a coater then applies the coatings and dries the paper.

For glossy magazine pages, the paper must be coated with compounds like clay, calcium carbonate, and latex.

To make paper with that recognizable gloss, the sheet must be sent through pressurized, heated rollers. Known as calendaring, this gives the paper a glossy, shiny finish.

The treated pulp is then spread over a fast-moving belt of mesh wire. Here, water starts being removed and the wood fibers begin fusing together, forming a long sheet.

Our magazine paper is finished! After being packaged, it gets shipped to magazine printers.

Then, the paper makes its way to the press. The sheet moves over an absorbent material and through heavy rollers that squeeze out even more water.

The finished paper is then spun into a massive roll known as a reel. If not being coated, the papermaking process is now complete!

Once the magazines have been read, they either end up in the trash or can be recycled!

The sheet is then dried with steam heat, sucking out any remaining moisture from the paper.

Paper pulp is the raw material from which sheets of paper are made.

to recycle because of the thin plastic coating on the inside that allows the cups to hold liquid) to our fast food burger wrappers (which are hard to recycle because of the metallic or wax coating). Once consumers send us these materials we recycle them through an advanced technology called hydro-pulping, whereby the coatings—the plastic from the coffee cup, or the metal from the burger wrapper—are removed, leaving the paper fibers, which can then be recycled into new paper.

On the other side we have been able to take a wide range of fibrous materials, from used denim and bed sheets to elephant poo and coffee husks, and shred them to turn them into paper. While these new paper forms are a bit more expensive, as they do not yet have the massive scale of the established paper industry, they create a unique and sometimes a bit comical (especially when we're making poo paper) alternative to using fiber from trees. We've even transformed old waxy paper (the paper board in which tomatoes and other vegetables are shipped to supermarkets) into eco-friendly fire logs (the wax creates a fantastic flame accelerator, limiting the need for classic petroleum brick fire logs). The possibilities are endless, especially when you change your perspective from waste being entirely negative to perhaps having some value.

With all this said, the real answer isn't as much how to recycle paper waste, although we should recycle as much as possible, nor is it how to make paper products more environmentally friendly, although that is also better than buying regular paper. The real answer is to stop using paper products altogether. Register with services that stop junk mail from going to your home. Resist printing something unless it's absolutely necessary. Try to bring a reusable cup to your favorite coffee shop instead of buying your coffee in a disposable paper cup. View your favorite newspaper digitally rather than getting the print edition delivered to your door. When asked if you want your groceries packaged in paper or plastic, say neither! In other words, stop using your hard-earned dollars to encourage more paper production. We do want to note that this book (assuming you are not reading an electronic version) was made using paper; when you're finished reading and using it, you can pass it along: give it to a friend or donate it to your local library.

WHAT YOU CAN DO
You can help reduce some stress on the waste stream by knowing the dos and don'ts of proper recycling (see Three Ways You're Not Recycling Paper Correctly and How to Change, page 98).

Are your old photographs recyclable? Find out by trying to rip them in half—if they tear like regular paper, they were printed and not exposed to chemical agents common to photographs. Most

Europe as a whole has the highest paper recycling rate of any region in the world at about 72%.

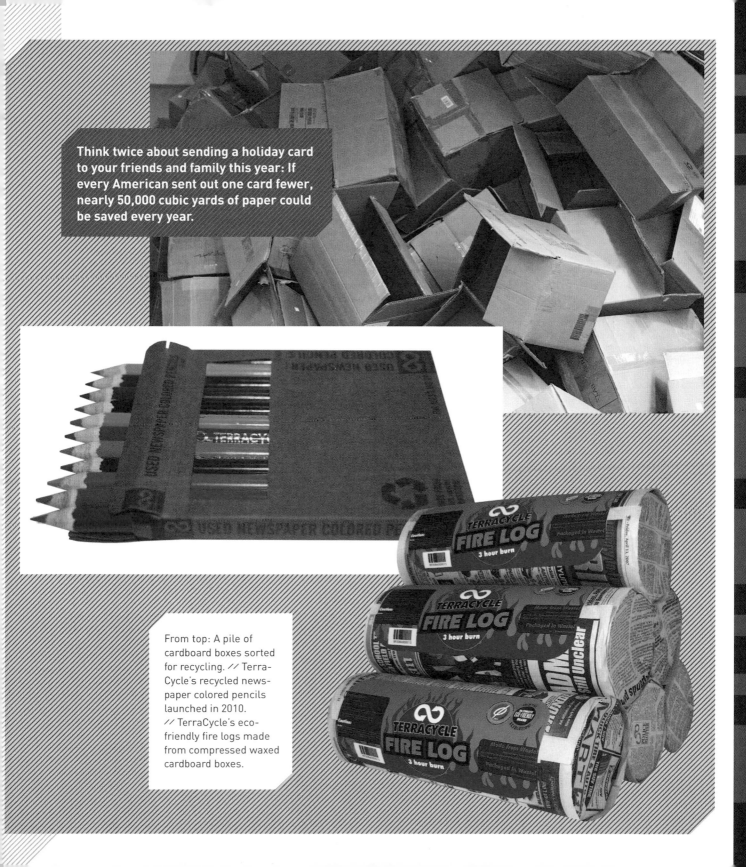

Think twice about sending a holiday card to your friends and family this year: If every American sent out one card fewer, nearly 50,000 cubic yards of paper could be saved every year.

From top: A pile of cardboard boxes sorted for recycling. // Terra-Cycle's recycled newspaper colored pencils launched in 2010. // TerraCycle's eco-friendly fire logs made from compressed waxed cardboard boxes.

RECORD ALBUM COVER JOURNAL

Vintage records can often be found in thrift stores and basements, but rarely get played. Dust off your favorite album cover and transform it into your own personal journal that is sure to be one of your greatest hits. For ages 12 and up.

WHAT YOU NEED

- Record album cover
- 30 sheets of 8½ x 11-inch paper
- Embroidery floss or dental floss
- Needle
- Scissors
- Ruler
- ⅛-inch hole punch
- Pencil

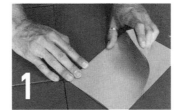

1 Fold your pages in half and open them back up. Stack the pages into six groups of five. Fold in half again.

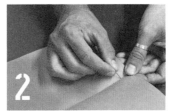

2 Using your needle, pierce holes every inch along the centerfold of each paper stack, starting ⅝ inch from the top.

TIP: USE SCRAP PAPER THAT HAS ONLY BEEN PRINTED ON ONE SIDE FOR THE PAGES INSIDE YOUR JOURNAL.

3 Cut the record album cover to two 5¾ x 8¾-inch pieces.

4 Using the ⅛-inch hole punch, punch holes every inch, starting ⅝ inch down from the top and ½ inch from the left.

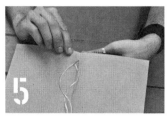

5

Double thread the needle with the floss. Tie a double knot at the end. Thread the floss through the inside bottom hole of one group of folded papers.

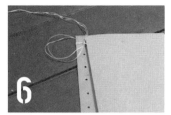

6

Thread through the bottom hole of the outside of the back cover. Loop your thread around the strand from group the of folded papers and gently pull tight.

7

Continue threading and looping your needle and thread through the remaining holes, connecting the group of folded papers to the back cover.

8

When you've reached the last hole in this first set, bring your needle through the outside top hole in the next group of folded papers. Then, thread through the next inside hole and loop your thread around the binding stitch that is already in place. Continue threading and looping through the remaining holes.

9

Continue this same method with three more groups of folded papers until they are all connected.

10

Place your last group of folded papers and the cover onto the top of the bound papers. Thread through the top of the front cover. Then, loop your thread through the binding stitch that is already in place.

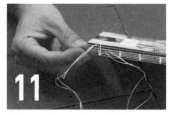

11

Thread through the outside hole in the last set of folded papers. Bring your needle and thread through the next inside hole and loop your thread around the binding stitch.

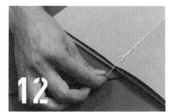

12

Continue threading and looping through the cover and then through the paper stack until the last stack of pages and cover are connected. For your last stitch, thread your needle from the outside of the group of folded

FINISHED

papers, with the thread ending in the centerfold. Double knot your thread and gently pull until tight. Trim off the end.

Above: Stacks of ubiquitous pizza boxes. // Opposite: Elephant dung can be turned into an eco-friendly paper.

1 **Trying to Recycle Soiled Paper Products:** Soiled paper products, i.e. paper towels, napkins, plates, and coffee filters, are not recyclable. The food scraps and grease contaminate the fibers and cause issues during the pulping process of papermaking (see below).

What to Do: Food-stained paper cannot be recycled, but it can be composted. Of the average 35 million tons of American waste, 32 percent is compostable.

2 **Shredding Paper Documents:** When done correctly, a single piece of white paper can be recycled up to eight times. By shredding the document, the paper fibers are shortened, drastically reducing the value and lifespan. Often, paper mills will not even accept shredded fragments.

What to Do: Avoid shredding entire documents. Rip off the confidential section of the paper for shredding. When you have to shred, bag shredded scraps separately from larger scraps and full-size pages to cut down the difficulties of sorting.

3 **Recycling Greasy Pizza Boxes:** Sure, the cardboard vessel is, in itself, recyclable. When laced with leftover grease, cheese, and sauce, it is a different story. During the recycling process, cardboard and paper is mixed with water. Any oil or food scraps upsets the binding of fibers in the pulping process and can ruin a whole batch of recycled paper.

What to Do: Before recycling, tear off any grease-stained portions of the box. Be sure to look for any stickers or advertisements; the adhesive causes similar recycling issues as oil.

municipal recycling centers that can process mixed paper will be able to reprocess them. If you can see multiple, separate layers after the tear (like a Polaroid), it's likely been coated with a variety of different substances, complicating the recycling process. To prevent these from ending up in the garbage, you should use old photographs in a craft or upcycled art project.

Paperenvironment.org is a great resource to check out when you want to learn about forest-related wood products, especially paper, and their environmental impact. The website is operated by the National Council for Air and Stream Improvement, a nonprofit that researches various environmental aspects of industries that require wood or forest-source materials to manufacture their products. An extensive, interactive infographic on the homepage diagrams every aspect of the paper

FOUR THINGS YOU DIDN'T KNOW PAPER COULD BE MADE OF

Today's paper is typically crafted from two sources: wood and recycled paper. But there are quite a few alternative raw materials that can be used to make paper, and some of them will likely surprise you.

1 **Elephant Poop:** The Alternative Pulp & Paper Company and Mr. Ellie Pooh have created recycled and odorless paper products sourced from animal waste. The process begins with fibers found in excretion from elephants, cows, horses, donkeys, and Thai buffalos. These animals have high-fiber diets of grass, bamboo, banana trees, twigs, and other vegetation. The fibers aren't completely broken down in the digestion process, leaving a significant amount to be sourced for paper. The poo fibers are boiled into pulp and mixed with non-fiber materials such as corn stalks, pineapple husks, banana tree trunks, and mulberry bark to form a strong paper material. The resulting mixture is screened and dried into its final paper stage.

2 **Plants and Husks:** The fibers from most plants can be transformed into paper products. Hemp is considered one of the best alternatives to typical wood paper. Hemp requires no bleaching, allowing the process to be chemical-free. It is not only stronger than regular paper, but also does not crack, yellow, or deteriorate. In addition to hemp, the husks of corn and coconut are viable tree-free alternatives to paper pulp.

3 **Straw:** "Agricultural residue" is a term used for straw left over from food grain harvesting, animal bedding, and water retention. This surplus is typically disposed of by burning, but in recent endeavors, has been used to create straw paper. Straw is a low-carbon option that creates half the ecological footprint of typical paper, and can save up to 550 to 830 million trees a year. India and China are leaders in producing straw paper, with 20 percent of their paper coming from wheat straw, rice straw, and sugarcane stalks.

4 **Coffee Bean Bags:** The U.S imports millions of sacks of coffee beans, leaving millions of burlap bags without a use. Whiting Paper Company, a paper mill in Wisconsin, works with these leftover bags to create Kona Paper, a sepia-colored paper made of fine ground burlap mixed with recycled non-burlap pulp. This process mimics the papermaking process of the past, when used rags were the raw material for paper production.

industry and how it affects the environment. There are videos, detailed information about how recycled paper fibers are reused, and even the impact chlorinating paper has on surrounding ecosystems.

If you want to get rid of books, donate them to your local library, or check out the website of the American Library Association (ala.org). While they don't do any donation or recycling programs directly, they do offer resources and databases to help find organizations that accept donations.

And please don't throw that greasy pizza box into your paper recycling bin.

Synthetic fabrics start from a substance made from coal, oil, or natural gas. The liquid passes through fine holes of a nozzle, called a spinneret. Then, the liquid cools and solidifies into threads.

CHAPTER 4

TEXTILES

There was once a time when clothes were simply tools of survival, providing warmth and protection against the elements in a world without electric heaters and down jackets. Today, it's a different situation. Some of us have dozens of pairs of shoes, one for every possible occasion. Others wear an outfit once, and then throw it away for fear of being considered "unfashionable." Instead of valuing durability and quality, many consumers are turning to fashion trends designed to be obsolete in a few months.

Factory farms, where cattle and other livestock are confined to produce things like milk, leather, meat, and fur, are responsible for 37% of all methane emissions in the U.S.

But despite all of the thought we put into our clothes, we rarely think about where they come from—not the designer label but the actual textiles that make up our clothes, the materials that are the building blocks of our favorite outfits. Why does the fashion industry use particular materials? What is the history of these materials? How does textile consumption affect our planet?

OUR FIRST CLOTHES

Scientists studying the evolution of head lice into body lice have estimated that humans began wearing animal pelts as clothing around 160,000 years ago. This coincides with the second-to-last ice age, showing that these furs were probably more for function than fashion. Scientists count this moment—up there with the controlled use of fire—as one of the most important factors in the progression of our species.

Jumping forward tens of thousands of years, humans began raising sheep for wool and food around 10,000 BCE. Wool continued to be an important source of material for clothing throughout the Middle Ages, gaining momentum with the help of the Black Death. Thanks to the sudden and dramatic decrease in the English population due to plague deaths, land became extremely cheap. Sheep farms became far more prevalent, and the region eventually grew to become one of the largest textile-producing nations in all of Europe.

Animals are far from the only source of textile materials. As early as 8000 BCE hemp was being

Previous spread: Piles of clothing in a landfill. Microscopic image of fabric threads (*inset*).
// Above: Animal pelt.
// Left: Early drawing of a medieval sheep pen and wool harvesting.

A flock of sheep after being sheared.

used to make cloth in Mesopotamia. Because of its association with marijuana, hemp tends to get a bad rap, but the plant is actually one of the earliest plants used to create fiber for textiles. Silk was another hugely influential textile. Gaining popularity in China around 1300 BCE, the opening of the famous Silk Road in 139 BCE allowed the material to spread across Asia and Europe. Cotton-based cloth was also brought to Europe through trade by Arab traders, around 800 CE. In fact, the word "cotton" comes from the Arabic word "qutun." Moving into Africa, linen was the material of choice for ancient Egyptians because it was a lightweight material. In 2920 BCE, the production of linen expanded as mummification became more common. Bodies were wrapped in linen as part of an extensive ritual meant to prepare the deceased for the afterlife. As we can see, textiles have always been more than just a means of clothing people. They represent status, ritual, and even the advancement of humanity. Pretty heavy stuff for a piece of cloth!

TEXTILE TECHNOLOGIES

With the advancement of textiles came advances in textile manufacturing technology. The first textile hand loom made its way from Asia to the West around 6000 BCE. Flash forward to 200 CE, and the first thread-spinning wheels are built in Asia (probably India or China). These were the height of thread-spinning technology for quite some time. The next big development didn't come until the modern era. In 1769, an English barber and wigmaker, Richard Arkwright, invented a machine capable of spinning 96 strands of cotton thread at the same time.

Not to be outdone, in 1784 inventor Edmund Cartwright created a crude power loom, which mechanically wove thread into cloth. Though Cartwright went bankrupt and lost many of his looms in a fire, rumored to have been started by disgruntled handloom weavers who worried about the future of their business, his power looms were a huge advancement in the textile industry. Combined with Arkwright's machine, these two inventions allowed the rate of cloth production to speed up, making it easier and quicker to produce larger amounts of cloth. While the loom was evolving, the cotton industry was also slowly growing, particularly in the U.S.

A MACHINE THAT CHANGED THE INDUSTRY (AND OUR NATION)

In 1794, the inventor Eli Whitney patented the cotton gin, a machine that revolutionized the cotton industry. Although cotton was easy to grow, it was difficult to separate the cotton seeds from the usable fibers. Until the cotton gin, the seeds and the fibers would have to be separated by hand, which took so long that the average cotton picker could only clean about one pound of cotton a day. The gin could separate the two easily and quickly, turning out close to 50 pounds of cotton a day. While this helped the South become a leader in the cotton industry, producing two-thirds of the world's cotton, this success story had a much

Right: Sure these chunks of chocolate look tasty, but did you know you could wear them as clothing? // Opposite: Linen-wrapped mummy.

FIVE BIZARRE MATERIALS USED TO MAKE CLOTHING

Cotton, leather, wool, synthetic fiber, balloons, toilet paper—wait, what? That's right, a few innovative designers from around the world have stepped beyond the conventional textile materials we're all used to, venturing into a wacky world of fashion.

1 Toilet Paper: Believe it or not, a company called Cheap-Chic-Weddings runs an annual Toilet Paper Wedding Dress contest, where designers attempt to make the best toilet paper wedding dress with hopes of winning a $10,000 grand prize.

2 Chocolate: No, we're not kidding. Spanish designer Paco Rabanne actually designs dresses made out of chocolate. How they don't melt on the runway, we have no clue.

3 Iron: These aren't suits of medieval armor we are talking about here. Designer Luana Jardim's Specular Collection is fashion made entirely out of iron and iron materials. It's one of the only articles of clothing that requires a welder instead of a seamstress.

4 Balloons: Designer Rie Hosokai from Japan makes dresses with this strange material in her "Daisy Balloon" collection.

5 Wedding Cake: Designer Lukka Sigurdardottir must have compared notes with Paco Rabanne, because Sigurdardottir also makes confectionary fashion, this time with wedding cake. Practical? No. Absolutely delicious? Definitely.

Cotton is used in everything from textile products such as shirts, jeans, sheets, and towels to fishnets, tents, and coffee filters; the cottonseed can be made into cooking oils and salad dressing.

The finest clothing made is a person's own skin, but, of course, society demands something more than this.
— MARK TWAIN

DENIM EYEGLASS CASE

If you are looking for an upcycled, stylish way to protect your glasses, reuse a pair of your favorite old jeans and make this eyeglass case! The inner lining adds to the protection, and it even includes extra pockets for things like keys and a cell phone. For ages 12 and up.

WHAT YOU NEED

- Pair of worn jeans
- Article of worn clothing, like a T-shirt, pajamas, or shirt, for the lining
- Zipper, 6 inches or longer
- Thread
- Sewing machine
- Pins
- Seam ripper
- Chalk or erasable fabric marker
- Scissors

TIP: USING THE POCKET OF JEANS ADDS A UNIQUE LOOK, JUST AVOID THE THICKER, STITCHED AREA.

Cut two 8¼ x 4¾-inch rectangles from the pair of jeans

Remove one of the belt loops using a seam ripper. Fold it in half and sew this onto the right side of one of the denim pieces about 1¼ inches down from the top edge.

Cut two 8¼ x 4¾-inch rectangles from the T-shirt, pajamas, or shirt.

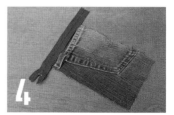
Place one of the denim pieces faceup. Then, along the upper width, place the zipper along the edge, wrong side up and centered over the fabric.

5

Take one of the lining pieces, and lay it on top of the zipper and denim, facedown. All three pieces (denim, zipper, lining) should align at the top, with the zipper sandwiched in the middle. Pin in place, and sew the two fabric pieces to the zipper.

6

Flip the sewn lining and denim to the face side.

7

Lay the remaining denim piece faceup. Turn the sewn section over so that the zipper pull is now on the opposite side but still facing down, and align the open side of the zipper with the denim. Place the remaining lining fabric on top of the entire set, facedown. Align the fabric pieces at the top of the zipper, with the pieces already sewn in the middle of the fabric sandwich and hanging slightly below.

8

Flip the second side of the sewn lining faceup. The lining pieces will fall on one side and the denim pieces on the other side. The right sides should be facing each other.

9

Unzip the zipper about halfway. Fold the zipper just a bit, so that the edges overlap. Pin in place around the three sides, and sew a continuous seam all the way around the entire case, beginning and ending with the lining. Be certain to leave an opening for turning.

10

Clip the excess zipper at the sides, then turn the pouch right side out by pulling everything through the opening. Use a pair of scissors to push out the corners of the outer fabric.

11

Sew the opening closed and tuck the lining inside of the pouch.

FINISHED

darker underbelly. As plantation owners found themselves capable of producing more usable cotton a day, they began planting more cotton plants.

More slaves were needed to maintain the cotton fields, and the southern economy became more reliant on them as a source of labor and revenue. With their lucrative cotton industry too closely intertwined with the fate of slavery, many historians trace the bloodshed of the Civil War back to the creation of Whitney's machine.

MAN-MADE TEXTILES

The year 1884 brought about a game-changing discovery in the textile industry. A French chemist named Count Hilaire de Chardonnet was working to help the French silk industry combat an epidemic killing silkworms, when he accidentally spilled a bottle of nitrocellulose. As he was cleaning up his mess, he realized that the nitrocellulose became viscous due to evaporation, and left behind strands of fibers that looked like silk. This one moment of clumsiness led to the invention of artificial silk, today known as rayon. Sure, the initial product was so flammable that an outfit made of the artificial silk reportedly burst into flames around a lit cigarette, but it was a start.

Did you know that the Wright Brothers used cotton to cover the wings of their aircraft in 1903 for their first powered flight?

In 1910, DuPont, a company that was previously known for its work with dynamite and powders, introduced an artificial leather they called Fabrikoid. The artificial leather was produced by coating fabric with nitrocellulose. Rather than using this new textile for clothing, however, Fabrikoid became the preferred choice for upholstery, luggage, and particularly convertible-car tops.

The production of rayon led to other breakthroughs, most notably the creation of nylon in 1938. It was the world's first true synthetic fiber, created entirely from chemicals. Initially it was marketed as a replacement for silk, particularly for women's stockings, but later use expanded to everything from clothing to tire cordage. The idea of using synthetic fabric to create clothing

Left: Portrait of Richard Arkwright, inventor of the thread-spinning machine (shown in painting). // Right: A modern home-made loom. // Opposite: Cotton field.

I guess the big thing is that I don't buy anything first-hand. It's a personal policy I have for all sorts of reasons. If you research the textile industry yourself, you'll know why. I came to it personally.

— EZRA MILLER

Right: Hilaire de Chardonnet, inventor of artifical silk. // Far right: Fleece, a modern synthetic textile, found in millions of closets worldwide.
// Below: A molecular bond in synthetic fibers.

quickly spread. After James Dickson and J. Rex Whinfield discovered polyethylene terephthalate in 1941, the two produced and patented a polyester fabric they called Terylene or Dacron. In the later 1940s DuPont licensed this fabric and saw its success throughout the years as a component of wash-and-wear fabrics. Just a few years later, in 1959, a DuPont employee named Joseph Shivers developed Spandex, known by DuPont as "Lycra." This fiber was more resistant to wear-and-tear than other fabrics, and its elastic qualities (it could stretch up to six times its original length) was perfect for clothes that benefited from a little bit of stretch.

DuPont wasn't having all of the fun with synthetics, of course. The American company Polartec, originally named Malden Mills Industries, created its first synthetic "polar fleece" in 1979. The product was meant to mimic natural, warm, soft sheep fleece, even though it's often made entirely from petroleum-sourced plastic. The product revolutionized the way cold-weather clothing was constructed to such a degree that *Time* magazine named polar fleece one of the 100 most important inventions of the twentieth century.

TEXTILE WASTE
We humans are buying more clothing every year. In 2000 alone, the world's consumers spent about $1 trillion on clothing. While this is great for the textile and fashion business, this isn't

so great for the earth. Because of constantly changing trends, consumers are not only buying more clothing, but they're throwing away more as well. In 2006, consumers in the U.K. averaged about 60 pounds of clothing and textile waste per capita per year; this waste ended up in landfills. Globally, about 7.5 billion pounds of clothing is landfilled each year.

Recycling and reusing textile waste helps mitigate some of our wastefulness. In 2005, for example, approximately 15 percent of Americans bought from thrift and secondhand stores. In 2006, Goodwill generated $1.8 billion by selling used goods, including secondhand clothing. Between the market for reused clothing and textiles recovered from the solid waste stream, Americans help divert around 2.5 billion pounds of textile waste from landfills every year.

Roughly 860,000 tons of clothes continue on in the international secondhand clothing market, often being shipped from the U.S. to developing countries in Africa and Asia. This can be a good thing in developing regions that lack money and

Synthetic textiles are strong, cheap, easy to care for, readily available, abrasion-resistant, resistant to moths and fungi, and have a low absorbency.

Wool is reusable and biodegradable! It can be turned into sweaters and then at the end of its life, it decomposes into the soil releasing valuable nutrients.

Above, left: Sheep's wool. // Above: Piles of unwanted clothing. // Below: Used clothing in a landfill.

resources, but can also strangle local clothing markets due to the dirt-cheap prices.

It isn't just the textiles themselves that are the problem. The energy exerted and resources used to make textiles are an entirely different problem. Clothing made of plastic fibers don't typically break down in the environment, which is a huge problem considering how much of it ends up being landfilled. It isn't a matter of choosing natural over synthetic fibers, or vice versa. We must instead find a way to work with both to clean up the textile industry, and, by extension, the planet.

TEXTILES TODAY

So, you need to buy a new shirt. You head to the mall and find that, besides considering style, you have a large number of material choices to consider. Should you buy a shirt made out of cotton or a synthetic fiber? Is wool more environmentally friendly than leather? If you're shopping with the planet in mind, making the eco-friendly choice isn't as easy as you may think.

The problem with fibers, both natural and synthetic, is that there's no quick fix. No one fiber is necessarily better for the planet than another. Instead, they all come with a list of pros and cons that we need to take into consideration when making purchases.

COTTON

Cotton accounts for nearly half of the fibers used to make clothes and textiles worldwide, as well as about 90 percent of all natural fibers used. About 90 different countries produce about 20 million tons of cotton every year. Cotton's an all-natural

TEXTILES TIMELINE

6000 By now, the first textile hand looms likely made their way into the West from Asia.

139 China opens the Silk Road, bringing valuable Chinese silk from eastern Asia all the way into what is now modern Turkey.

168,000 BCE By studying when head lice began evolving into body lice, scientists approximate that by this time early humans began wearing animal hide and fur clothing.

3000 Dyes for textiles like wool originate roughly around this time in Mesopotamia, mostly using pomegranate and other organics.

200 CE The first thread-spinning wheels are built in parts of Asia, most likely in India or China.

900 Historical records suggest that the first true windmills start to appear, revolutionizing the way humans produce commodities like corn, flour, and textiles.

10,000 Humans in many parts of the world have started raising sheep for wool and food.

2920 While evidence suggests cloth production began in Egypt at an earlier time, it expanded significantly around now when mummification was more widely practiced.

800 Cotton-based cloth spreads throughout Europe by Arab traders. The word "cotton" is even derived from the Arabic "qutun."

1352 With land so cheap following the Black Death pandemic, sheep farms become more prevalent throughout Europe, setting the stage for a new wool industry.

1300 Silk production takes off in China, but it will be another thousand years or so before the silk trade finally reaches Europe.

1769 Richard Arkwright invents a machine capable of spinning 96 strands of cotton thread at the same time.

8000 Hemp, one of the earliest plants used to create fiber for textiles, is grown for cloth in Mesopotamia.

1784 Edmund Cartwright invents the power loom, which mechanically weaves thread into cloth. Combined with Arkwright's innovation, cloth production speeds begin to surge!

1794 The cotton gin is patented by inventor Eli Whitney, making it possible to efficiently separate seeds from cotton fibers after harvesting.

1860 Facilitated by slavery and the cotton gin, the southern U.S. states are producing two-thirds of all cotton in the world.

1884 Count Hilaire de Chardonnet of France invents an efficient process for manufacturing a synthetic fiber called rayon, still a widely used textile material today.

1938 Nylon, the first completely synthetic, chemically derived fiber, enters the market as a replacement for fibers in women's clothing.

1979 Synthetic polar fleece is manufactured by American company Polartec to mimic natural, warm, soft sheep fleece, even though it's often made entirely from petroleum-sourced plastic.

2000 People around the world bought one trillion dollars' worth of clothing.

1846 The first patent on a mechanical sewing machine is filed by American inventor Elias Howe.

1910 DuPont begins producing "artificial leather," or fabrics coated with synthetic nitrocellulose, a perfect material for luggage, convertible tops, and automobile seating upholstery.

1941 After the discovery of polyethylene terephthalate, James Dickson and J. Rex Whinfield invent polyester fabric.

1959 Spandex is developed by DuPont employee Joseph Shivers. Known by DuPont as Lycra, this synthetic fiber was resistant to wear-and-tear and perfect for clothes requiring a bit more stretch.

2006 As many as 15% of Americans make purchases at thrift stores each year, annually diverting an estimated 2.5 billion pounds of textile waste from landfills.

TODAY Only 16% of all textile products are recycled in the U.S.

material that doesn't harm animals. But this doesn't mean it's environmentally friendly. It takes about 700 gallons of water to make one cotton T-shirt. Cotton farming also accounts for 24 percent of insecticide and 11 percent of pesticide sales in the world.

SYNTHETIC FIBERS

Unlike natural fibers, synthetics aren't biodegradable, which means they'll sit in landfills forever. The production of them also comes with its own set of problems. Synthetic fibers rely on nonrenewable resources like oil. Making synthetic fibers also uses a lot of energy and often requires the fibers to be treated with various chemicals that aren't great for the planet.

LEATHER

Some of the downsides of leather are obvious. Animal rights activists have been calling for a leather boycott for years, claiming that the animals are often raised and killed under inhumane conditions. Even from a non–animal rights perspective there are definitely major issues with the leather industry. Turning animal skin into usable leather requires the hide to be treated with a ton of

TEN HOUSEHOLD TEXTILES YOU DIDN'T KNOW COULD BE RECYCLED OR REUSED

You probably know that you can donate just about any decent clothing to thrift and consignment shops like Goodwill for reuse. For more options you can visit weardonaterecycle.com, a website operated by the Council for Textile Recycling. There you will find a searchable database of locations and recyclers where you can bring old textile products you wouldn't normally think to recycle or donate. Here is a small list of what you could be diverting from the landfill:

1 **Stuffed animals**

2 **Entire bedding sets**

3 **Halloween costumes**

4 **Boots**

5 **Cloth napkins**

6 **Purses and handbags**

7 **Pillows**

8 **Curtains and drapes**

9 **Belts**

10 **Athletic jerseys**

While some municipal systems may accept some of these items, it is unlikely that most have the infrastructure in place to process them. It is important to always try to reuse or donate when possible, and recycle only as a last resort.

FIVE WAYS THE TEXTILE INDUSTRY AFFECTS THE ENVIRONMENT

1 It Is Heavily Reliant on Water: Making a cotton T-shirt requires as much as 700 gallons of water.

2 The Use of Toxic Dyes: Many textile manufacturers use dyes that release aromatic amines, or toxic organic compounds that can contain heavy metals, ammonia, alkali, toxic solids, and large amounts of pigment. These chemicals are hazardous to factory employees who work with them, and can even end up seeping into water supplies used by nearby residents.

3 Solid Waste Pollution: The textile industry is also responsible for the generation of large quantities of solid waste: scraps of fabric and yarn, packaging waste, empty chemical and dye containers, cardboard reels and cones, and fabric that didn't meet factory specifications.

4 Water Pollution: In addition to large water use, countless chemicals used to manufacture textiles risk polluting nearby water sources at every point of the production cycle. Cleaning and bleaching fibers, using dyes, washing finished products and disposing of waste water are all processes that risk pollution.

5 Air Pollution: Textile factories can emit greenhouse gases at many points during the manufacturing process—so much so that, next to water pollution, air pollution is one of the greatest environmental hazards caused by the textile industry.

Opposite, left: Pieces of leather for sale at an outdoor market. // Opposite, right: Display of donated stuffed animals. // Right: Wild cotton grass.

Organic cotton, which is grown without the use of synthetic fertilizers, pesticides, or herbicides, accounts for less than 1 percent of all cotton produced globally.

chemicals like arsenic sulfide and sodium hydroxide. In fact, the tanning process requires so many chemicals that the land around tanneries can become unusable, and its run-off can pollute local waterways.

WOOL

At first glance, wool seems like a fairly eco-friendly choice. It comes from a sustainable source and the sheep, unlike the less lucky cows, usually get to survive. Here's where the "but" comes in. The sheep are typically treated with insecticides and pesticides that are bad for both humans and the environment. There's also the problem of land usage. Sheep need to graze, and the more sheep you have, the more land you need to feed them. Argentina, which during the first half of the twentieth century was a major wool producer, found this out the hard way when its sheep population

decimated the land. Sheep also tend to produce a lot of methane, so much so that New Zealand calculates that 90 percent of its methane emissions come from its sheep. Turning their wool into usable fibers requires almost as much water as cotton, and the chemicals used in dyes are an environmental issue as well.

LOOKING FORWARD

If collected properly, textiles, from your pillowcase to your favorite dress, can be reused, upcycled, or even recycled; in fact, no textiles should ever end up in the garbage as they are full of value. At TerraCycle, to accomplish such circular processing, we run a wide range of collection programs for textiles from bringing clothing to drop points at your favorite retailers to providing mail-in programs where you can send them to us.

In developed countries, people typically discard their clothing due to changes in fashion trends, not because the clothing is threadbare and worn, so the vast majority of the textiles we collect are reused (simply cleaned and resold to developing countries). While it's great that reuse is the very best circular repurposing solution available to any waste stream, and the majority of the collected clothing can be reused, it does underscore the effect of fashion as a creator of waste. Just think about your closet and the number of garments you have that are perfectly fine, but won't be worn again because of changes in fashion.

Some of the textiles TerraCycle collects cannot be easily reused so they are upcycled by our design department through partnerships with other textile manufacturers. For example, in partnering with the U.S. Postal Service and Timbuk2, old mailbags that would normally be thrown away are turned into durable consumer products like messenger bags.

Above: A woman peruses a rack of new clothing.
// Opposite: An upcycled dress made from USPS mail bags on display at the TerraCycle offices.

Nature's first green is gold,
Her hardest hue to hold.
Her early leaf's a flower;
But only so an hour.
Then leaf subsides to leaf.
So Eden sank to grief,
So dawn goes down to day.
Nothing gold can stay.
— ROBERT FROST

SPORT COAT TOTE

A stained or torn sport coat is still perfectly suitable for this tote. Matching neckties dress up this bag and provide the fabric to make this project entirely upcycled. Once your project is complete, reuse the leftover scraps for your own inspiration. For ages 12 and up.

WHAT YOU NEED

- 1 to 2 old sport coats
- 2 worn neckties
- Thread
- ½-inch-wide bias tape
- Ruler
- Tailor's chalk or fabric marker
- Fabric scissors
- Iron
- Pins
- Sewing machine

Place your sport coat on a flat surface. Starting from the bottom edge, measure two 14-inch squares with a pocket inside the measured panel. Mark the squares with tailor's chalk.

Cut along the marked lines, making sure that you cut both the outer layer and inner lining of the coat and leaving the bottom, seamed edge intact.

Cut your neckties to 24 inches measuring from the narrow end of each necktie.

Iron 1 inch down from the top of each sport coat panel so that the right sides are facing out on both and the ends are tucked in. This will allow a clean, hemmed edge at the top of your tote.

5 Take one necktie and place each end 4 inches in from the outer edges of the coat panel. Sandwich the end of the necktie between the coat front and the lining. Pin in place.

6 Continue to pin along the top edge. Sew along this pinned edge, using a ¼-inch seam allowance. Repeat for the second panel.

7 With the right sides of the two coat panels facing together, pin along the sides and bottom edges. Using a ½-inch seam allowance, sew along the pinned edges.

8 Fold down the end of the bias tape by ½-inch. Then, pin bias tape, wrapping around the sewn together side edges to bind the edges and sew in place. This will keep your fabric from fraying.

9 To create box corners, flatten the body of the tote with the side seam laying flat on top of the bottom seam, creating a triangle with the corner of the fabric. Mark a line 1½ inches down from the corner and perpendicular to the seam.

10 Stitch a straight line along your marked line. Repeat for the other box corner. Flip your tote to the right side and your new bag is ready for business.

FINISHED

The little that cannot be reused or upcycled is then recycled by leveraging the fibers that the textile is made from. Through this process, natural textiles can be turned into paper, insulation, and a host of other materials. And synthetic textiles can be melted into a plastic polymer that can then be used to make just about any plastic product you can imagine.

As with every waste stream, the true answer isn't just proper collection and repurposing. Instead the answer is choosing to buy smarter. Try to buy timeless, used, and, ideally, fewer garments. This will not only help save the environment but also send a strong signal to the fashion industry to change its approach to quality and trends.

WHAT OTHERS ARE DOING

Scientists, bloggers, and nonprofit organizations are looking for ways to improve the textile industry and educate the public on how to dress more sustainably.

Focusing on reforming the fashion industry from the inside, the Ethical Fashion Forum, a non-profit dedicated to transforming social and environmental standards in the fashion industry, launched

Cotton is a good conductor of heat, which means it keeps the body cool in the summer and warm in the winter.

Opposite: Rhino Mail, a rhinoceros made from upcycled canvas USPS mail bags, by Ede Sinkovics. // Left: A display of upcycled clothing and accessories from the Terra-Cycle offices. // Below: Office chairs upholstered with upcycled men's suits.

Wool has a variety of uses: from making fire-resistant products to sound proofing and climate control, clothing, upholstery, carpeting, and more.

SOURCE in 2011. SOURCE aims to be a resource for those in all areas of the fashion industry, helping them advertise their own environmentally responsible products. Consumers can also use the site to locate brands and shops that carry clothes that are eco-friendly and socially responsible.

WHAT YOU CAN DO

There are easy ways to shop responsibly, which include buying clothes used from thrift and consignment shops. You can also donate your old clothing to these shops to save them from being landfilled. If you do choose to buy your clothing new, look for items made from better-quality fabrics. Well-made pieces may cost a little more, but they'll last a lot longer than a cheaper version that will fall apart after the first few washings.

Like most things "eco," the material itself is hardly the only problem. Think about how you're washing and drying your clothing, too. Are you washing your clothes more often than is necessary? Are you washing a load even if your hamper isn't full? Cutting back on how many loads of laundry you do can dramatically reduce your energy usage and carbon footprint. Dryers use electricity to generate heat, and about three-quarters of the carbon footprint per wash is from the drying process. Try switching to a drying rack or a clothesline and letting nature take care of your clothes instead.

LIFECYCLE OF JEANS

Four to five months after being planted on large plantations, ready-to-harvest cotton is picked with a "cotton stripper" machine and pressed into truck-sized, rectangular blocks called modules.

The lint is pressed into cotton bales weighing over 500 pounds. The bales are sold to a local buyer, who ships them to a spinning mill.

At the mill, the cotton goes into a carding machine, which further cleans the cotton and straightens it into soft rope called slivers.

Looms tightly weave the "warp" (lengthwise) and the "weft" (horizontal) threads into a diagonal pattern called a twill weave. The blue cotton thread is woven together with white cotton thread to give jeans their color. Other components such as polyamide, polyester, and nylon are also sometimes woven in for flexibility and durability.

The modules or bales are transported to a cotton gin, where machines separate the cottonseed and other waste from the raw cotton fiber, or lint.

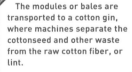

Spinning frames then twist the fibers into thread, which is dyed blue with synthetic indigo.

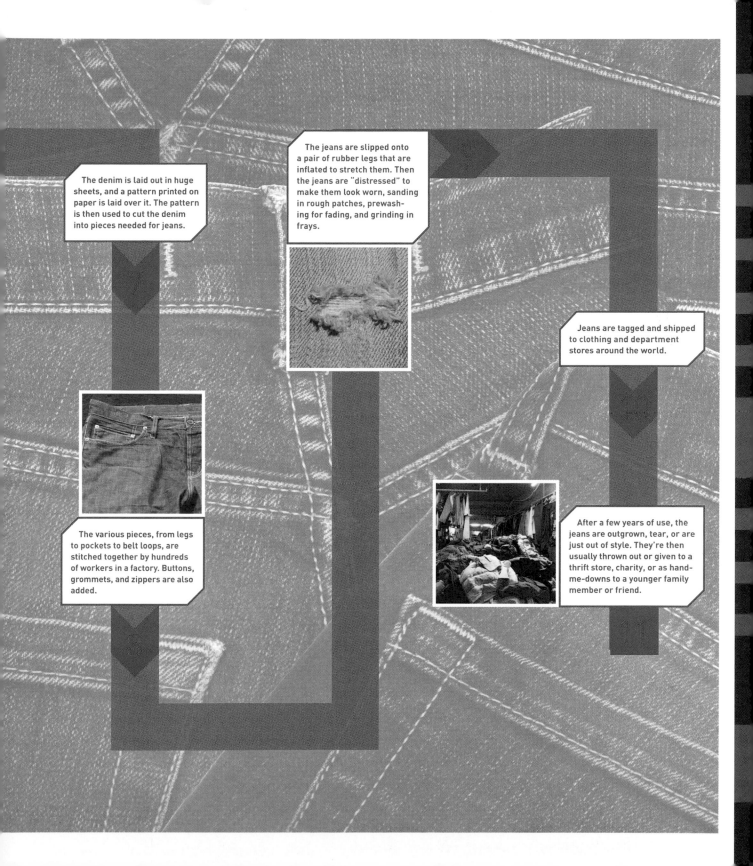

The denim is laid out in huge sheets, and a pattern printed on paper is laid over it. The pattern is then used to cut the denim into pieces needed for jeans.

The jeans are slipped onto a pair of rubber legs that are inflated to stretch them. Then the jeans are "distressed" to make them look worn, sanding in rough patches, prewashing for fading, and grinding in frays.

Jeans are tagged and shipped to clothing and department stores around the world.

The various pieces, from legs to pockets to belt loops, are stitched together by hundreds of workers in a factory. Buttons, grommets, and zippers are also added.

After a few years of use, the jeans are outgrown, tear, or are just out of style. They're then usually thrown out or given to a thrift store, charity, or as hand-me-downs to a younger family member or friend.

There are great websites like Eco Friendly Fashion (ecofriendly-fashion.com), which connects conscious consumers with companies that focus on sustainability and eco-friendly materials. Ecouterre (ecouterre.com) provides the latest news in eco-fashion, developments in the textile industry, and DIYs for the crafty. These companies, nonprofits, and resources offer exciting solutions, but there's always more that must be done. Buy clothes from thrift stores, reuse old textiles when you can, and always donate your clothing instead of throwing it out — an old blanket today, an upcycled tablecloth tomorrow.

Do your research before giving certain brands of clothing your money, as some have been responsible for horrifying damage to ecosystems around the world. Limit what you purchase to only the necessities, while buying more durable products. You'll save money in the long run when you buy something that will be a part of your wardrobe for years, not months.

Blue Jeans Go Green™

BLUE JEANS GO GREEN is a recycling program that has collected more than 1 million pieces of denim and has diverted more than 600 tons of denim waste out of landfills. The program was initiated by Cotton Incorporated in 2006 in an effort to ease the environmental burden caused by jean production, and to improve local communities through UltraTouch Denim Insulation. Habitat for Humanity is one recipient of Ultra-Touch Insulation; in 2012 nearly 250,000 square feet of it was given to the organization's affiliates across the U.S.

The process begins with consumers, who send their old jeans to Blue Jeans Go Green. The denim is reverted into cotton fibers — the first step in the insulation-making process. The cotton fiber is then treated with chemicals that make it fire-retardant and resistant to mold. Finally, the sheets of insulation are cut to size, packaged, shipped, and installed in homes and buildings. Partnerships with clothing retailers like G by Guess, Gap, Rock & Republic, True Religion, and American Eagle have helped collect even more.

To get involved, you can visit the organizations's website at bluejeansgogreen.org/Get-Involved/.

Left: An upcycled purse made from old denim blue jeans. // Right: Recycling symbol upcycled from various textiles. // Opposite: Polluted river.

Those who contemplate the beauty of the earth find reserves of strength that will endure as long as life lasts. There is something infinitely healing in the repeated refrains of nature—the assurance that dawn comes after night, and spring after winter.

—RACHEL CARSON, *Silent Spring*

Glass is what's known as a "fourth state of matter"—it looks like a liquid on a molecular level, but has the hardness and rigidity of a solid.

CHAPTER 5

GLASS

The story of glass begins tens of thousands of years ago with the development of glass's earliest ancestor, ceramic. Our ancestors discovered that clay, when heated in a hot oven, turned into a hard, rigid material perfect for making objects like small figurines and vessels.   Just like that, the ceramic industry was born. Archaeologists have found human and animal figurines left behind by these ancient artists, who fired them in kilns partially dug into the ground. Our oldest examples of pottery came just a little bit later, around 18,000 BCE in China.

There had previously been debate over whether pottery originated in Japan or China, but a recent search at Yuchanyan in China's Hunan province uncovered bits of pottery that outdated anything found so far. These fragments date to around the end of the last ice age, which suggests that pottery was used for cooking way before farming reached that part of the world.

We're pretty confident about the beginnings of ceramics, but glass is another story. Natural glass, which comes from lightning striking sand, volcanic activity, and meteorites, had been around for quite a while and was used for everything from spear tips to jewelry. It's still unclear, however, when and where man-made glass began. Historian Pliny the Elder of ancient Rome wrote that glass was discovered accidentally by traders in Syria around 5000 BCE. The story goes that a group of traders from Phoenicia (an ancient civilization in what is now Lebanon and Syria) stopped in the Syrian desert to cook some food, using blocks of nitrate to place their kettles on. The heat actually melted the nitrate, which combined with the surrounding desert sand. When it cooled, the mixture solidified into glass.

Whether or not Pliny was correct in naming the origins of glass, the earliest archaeological evidence of man-made glass objects dates about 5,000 years ago. Around 4000 to 3000 BCE, glass began being produced in the form of a glaze on ceramic vessels and stone beads. It is speculated that glass was discovered at this time, again by accident, when ancient potters overheated their kilns, producing a glassy glaze on their ceramic objects. By 1500 BCE the first glass vessels were produced in Egypt and Mesopotamia, created by covering a core of sand with a layer of molten glass.

In addition to lightning, volcanic activity can create glass when lava fuses rock and sand to form obsidian.

When a pane of glass cracks, the cracks can move across the surface as fast as 3,000 miles per hour.

Ancient clay pots excavated from the ruins of Chersonese in modern-day Crimea.

This spurred a rapid 300-year increase in the glass industry, followed by a couple of hundred years of decline. The reason for the decline is not entirely known, but a clear lack of historical and archaeological evidence of glass or glassmaking during this time suggests that ancient civilizations stopped making glass altogether for several hundred years.

Glassmaking was revived in Mesopotamia in the 700s BCE and in Egypt in the 500s BCE. In the next 500 years, Egypt, Syria, and other countries along the eastern shore of the Mediterranean became glassmaking centers. It wasn't an easy business, though. It was slow, costly, and neither the furnaces nor the clay pots were sufficient for creating quality glass. But, with a little persistence, the ancients were able to create products worthy of the upper class (the only ones who could afford it). Glass became the preferred means of transporting things like wine, honey, and oil. Around 50 BCE glassmakers' jobs got a little easier. The blow pipe was invented somewhere along the Mediterranean coast, making glass production easier, faster, and, most important, cheaper. Suddenly, glass wasn't just for priests and royalty, but was affordable for everyone. Glassmaking spread, becoming especially important to those under Roman rule.

STAINED AND CRISTALLO GLASS

In the first century CE, wealthy Romans used stained glass in their villas and palaces. These windows weren't considered art at the time, but rather domestic luxuries. That would all change in 313 CE, when Constantine allowed Christians to worship openly. The Christians began building churches based on Byzantine models, using Byzantine art as inspiration for the windows.

In 1996, the U.S. recycled 24.5% of discarded glass. In 2012, 27.7% — an increase of 3.2%.

The earliest surviving example of these windows is a Head of Christ from Lorsch Abbey in Germany, dated around the tenth century. As more churches were built throughout the ninth and tenth centuries, more stained glass started popping up as decoration for them. These stained-glass windows typically used blue, red, and white glass to let in as much light as possible into the dark churches.

It's the Venetians, though, who may be the most famous glassmakers even today. By the time the Crusades rolled around, Venice had already developed glass manufacturing, and by the 1290s an elaborate guild system of glassworkers had been set up. Venice became famous for its beautiful and delicate glasswork. In 1450, an Italian named Angelo Barovier invented *cristallo* glass, which is almost perfectly transparent, thin, and pliable due to a lack of impurities and a mixture of different compounds and chemical agents. The Venetians would improve on the cristallo glass, using it to make lacework patterns on things like goblets, bowls, and vases.

OPTICAL GLASS

Jumping forward 1,500 years, in 1590 the first optical lenses for the telescope and microscope were invented in the Netherlands. The English were working with glass as well. In 1674, the English glassmaker George Ravenscroft produced an entirely new kind of glass called lead glass. He introduced lead (hence the name) into the materials used during the glass-blowing process in order to prevent the clouding that sometimes occurred. This glass, which was softer and had a higher refractive index, would be utilized by the optical industry.

Let's turn now to what was happening with glasswork in America. The first glassmaking facility opened in 1608 in what would be the U.S. in Jamestown, Virginia. Though the English were producing some glass at home, many of their glass products had to be imported as industry began expanding into the surrounding forestland. As deforestation escalated in the country, the wood needed to fuel glass kilns became scarce. Luckily, the English had a bunch of new colonies with plenty of natural resources, which led to the

Glass naturally has a green tint and the thicker the piece of natural glass, the greener it appears.

If slaughterhouses had glass walls, everyone would be a vegetarian.
— PAUL MCCARTNEY

FIVE COOL TYPES OF GLASS YOU MAY NOT KNOW EXIST

There are many kinds of glass, capable of doing everything from killing bacteria to heating your home.

1 Heated: Companies have been making heated glass products for years. One manufacturer, Essex Security Glass (ESG), makes its own brand by sandwiching a chamber of argon gas between layers of glaze and a sheet of glass. When a current is applied (meaning it needs a power source), the gas actually starts generating heat right behind the glass. Windows like these can be installed in your own home or business as an extra source of heating, even if they are not very eco-friendly. Because the heat is being generated directly next to the exterior, the heat constantly risks seeping outside, wasting a lot of energy.

2 Metallic: Glass is strong, but it's not very tough. In other words, it can hold a lot of weight, but can't absorb much impact. Metallic glass made from palladium solves this problem. It can bend instead of shattering on impact, and is strong enough to hold a lot of weight. A strong glass like this has endless applications in aerospace, the military, or the automotive industry.

3 Antimicrobial: This glass kills bacteria not due to chemical coatings or treatments, but because of silver. It is imbued with silver ions that actually react with the cell membranes of bacteria, increasing their permeability and metabolism, causing the cell to generate toxic levels of oxygen until the bacteria eventually die. Tablet devices or glass objects that are handled by many people can benefit from antimicrobial glass, and hospitals already use antimicrobial surfaces to reduce the spread of bacteria.

4 Spray-on: This glass exists as a simple mixture of silicon dioxide (what regular glass is made of) and water or ethanol. It's antimicrobial, food safe, resistant to water, and stays flexible because the layer is 500 times as thin as a single hair. The spray could be applied to a shirt to make it waterproof, or to a surface to add a protective, antimicrobial glaze to it. Because it is safe and nontoxic, it can be used in a variety of ways.

5 Flexible: Glass is usually rigid and heavy, but the Corning glass company has developed a lightweight version that can actually be bent and shaped without shattering. Called Willow® Glass, it will likely start finding its way into smartphones and curved-screen electronics sometime within the next few years.

Above: One of the metallic mirrors recovered from the Genesis spacecraft in 2004.

The energy created when recycling one glass bottle can power a computer for a half hour, a 100-watt lightbulb for four hours, or a television for 20 minutes.

A modern glass-bottling production line.

creation of the first glass-manufacturing facility in the New World.

A couple of hundred years later in 1827, the American glassmaker Deming Jarves began experimenting with pressing, rather than blowing, glass. Though glass-pressing technology existed in Europe, it was still relatively new, unsophisticated, and pretty much unheard of in America. Jarves demonstrated that by dropping molten glass into a mold and pressing the plunger down, he could create an ornate glass tumbler. Another American development occurred in 1843, when Henry Bessemer developed one of the earliest instances of float glass. By pouring molten glass evenly onto a pool of liquid metal, Bessemer found that he could create a long, flat sheet with uniform thickness, perfect for windows.

GLASS BOTTLES AND SHATTERPROOF GLASS

Glassmaking technology and innovations continued to improve. In 1887 the glassmaking process became partially automated when a glassmaker in Castleford, Yorkshire, invented a machine capable of making 200 bottles per hour. That was more than three times faster than previous production methods. A few years later, in 1903, American Michael Owens formed the Owens Bottle Machine Company based on his own glassmaking machine. A former child laborer in a glass-bottle factory, Owens had been experimenting with a piston-pump that would suck molten glass into a mold and then transfer it into another mold where it was blown by reversing the pump. Each of his machines could be built with anywhere from six to twenty arms, with each blowing a bottle. This cut down on labor costs, since a fifteen-arm machine could do the work of at least a dozen skilled glassworkers. Owens continued to reinvent the glassmaking industry, retiring in 1919 with 45 U.S. patents.

The same year that Owens patented his machine, the French artist and chemist Édouard Bénédictus made a clumsy move and accidentally invented shatterproof glass. While using a ladder to reach for something on a shelf, he knocked a glass flask onto the floor. Instead of shattering, however, the glass more or less stuck together. Bénédictus realized that the flask had contained a type of liquid plastic that had left a thin film inside the flask that allowed it to hold together when dropped. This discovery came at the perfect time. Cars were becoming more popular in Paris, which meant that there were more car accidents. These accidents were made worse by flying glass shards from the broken windshields. Bénédictus ultimately created the safety glass that would grace the windshields of cars around the world.

FIBER OPTICS

Optical fiber technology, which uses light to send images and information through long strands of glass as thick as a human hair, started being developed around this time as well. Fiber optics essentially work by sending light signals through bundles of these hairlike pieces of glass. When the light is received at its destination, something called an optical receiver deciphers the information, and passes it along to whatever technology it was meant to reach, be it a personal computer or television set.

In the 1920s, a British inventor named John Baird patented an optical fiber system that would allow transparent rods to send images long distances. The biggest breakthrough didn't occur until the 1930s, when German physician Heinrich Lamm became the first to actually send an image via optical fibers. It wouldn't be until the 1970s

Glass was formed in nature before humans ever had a chance to manufacture it. Fulgurites (glass tubes) are created when lightning strikes sand.

that an efficient fiber-optic system would finally be developed by Corning, giving birth to the start of the optical fiber industry we know today.

Glass has been around for a really long time, has undergone a lot of developments, and can be used for a lot of different things. It magnifies microbes in the laboratory, provides eyesight to those losing their own, sends images to our television sets, protects homes from the elements, and is used in countless other ways. We owe quite a lot of our success as a civilization to this unassuming material, even if we aren't always aware it is right in front of our faces.

GLASS TODAY

Glass can be recycled over and over again without its quality and structural integrity diminshing. So why do we only recycle one third of our glass waste?

GLASS COLLECTION

The biggest issue with recycling glass currently is finding an efficient and user-friendly way to collect glass and bring it to a recycling center. The number one reason people give for not recycling is that it is "inconvenient." One in five Americans say they

Above: Two examples of fulgurites found in a desert in Mauritania. // Left: Traditional pottery kiln.

would recycle more if there were more convenient recycling bins.

Many programs in place have a number of requirements that discourage potential recyclers: you need to rinse and clean the glass, remove lids or caps, hand sort the glass by color, and personally drive it to the collection center. There are only 9,000 curbside collection programs in the U.S. to cover over 316 million people. Therefore, many people, especially in rural areas, do not receive the luxury of curbside recycling pick-up.

Why are we stretched so thin in the U.S.? The short answer is economics. Today, the rate at which materials are recycled is entirely dependent on economic and market incentive. If a municipality does not believe it will see enough of a return with a curbside recycling program, it simply won't invest in one. There can be a lot of incentives: maybe there is a glass recycling facility nearby that will buy recovered glass, or a local aluminum processing plant that will buy aluminum cans. The economic and market-driven demand for the collection of recyclable materials is almost always the deciding factor.

ENVIRONMENTAL IMPACT

There is no way to hide the environmental disadvantages of manufacturing new materials in general, let alone glass. To create brand new "virgin" glass, extremely high temperatures and a lot of energy are necessary. Temperatures of up to 3,000 degrees Fahrenheit are required in order to melt together silica sand, limestone, soda ash, and additional chemicals.

Glass has the quickest turnaround time of any other recycled material. It can go from a recycling bin back out onto store shelves in as few as 30 days.

As for greenhouse gas emissions, the combustion created by melting the raw materials releases carbon dioxide, sulfur dioxide, and nitrogen oxide. The biggest pollutant is carbon dioxide; for every two pounds of glass produced, more than one pound of carbon dioxide is emitted. With the current global production of glass at 135 million tons, that's 81 million tons of carbon dioxide pollution every year. Nitrogen oxide emissions vary depending on the type of glass produced. On average though, 16 pounds of nitrogen oxide are produced for every ton of glass. Using the same production number, that's close to 1 million tons of nitrogen oxide emitted. Finally, 5.5 pounds of sulfur dioxide is produced for every ton of glass manufactured; that's almost 340,000 tons of SO_2 per year.

The process of recycling glass into cullet (small, broken-down pieces of glass that can be used to make new products) uses much lower temperatures, using 40 percent less energy than new glass. It also emits much less pollution than creating new glass. When cullet use increases by 10 percent, it cuts carbon dioxide emission by 8 percent, nitrogen oxide by 4 percent, and sulfur oxides by 10 percent.

GLOBAL SCALE

Today, the global glass industry produces $75 billion in revenue every year. The top exporters around the world include Belgium, France, China, Germany, Japan, and the U.S. That's a lot of glass. So what happens with it?

It is estimated that 30 to 35 percent of container glass produced globally actually makes it into the recycling loop. That means that about 90 million tons of glass bottles and jars are sent to landfills around the world.

Europe is the world leader in recycling. Glass recycling, in particular, sees a significant difference between Europe and the rest of the world. Europe's high recovery rates are no coincidence.

GLASS TIMELINE

24,000 BCE Using holes in the ground as primitive kilns, early human beings make ceramic figurines out of clay.

1500 Glassmakers in Mesopotamia make glass using the core-forming technique, when a solid core of sand is dipped into molten glass, cooled, and finally cleaned of all dirt from the core.

50 The art of glassblowing is discovered on the coast of the Mediterranean, making glass more versatile, easier to produce, and cheaper for everyone.

1450 An Italian named Angelo Barovier invents "cristallo" glass, which is near-perfectly transparent due to a lack of impurities and a mixture of different compounds and chemical agents.

18,000 Shards of pottery found in China suggest that this is the earliest point in history where humans were making ceramic pottery.

650 The earliest instructions for glassmaking are written on tablets in Mesopotamia.

313 Constantine of Rome allows his subjects to practice Christianity. As the number of churches increases, stained glass rises to prominence as a means of artistic expression.

1590 The first optical lenses for microscopes and telescopes are invented in the Netherlands.

25 CE Porcelain is likely being crafted by now in China during the Han Dynasty.

1608 The first glassmaking facility on American soil is founded in Jamestown, Virginia.

2300 While natural glass from meteorites and volcanic activity was likely discovered earlier, glass is now finally being made by hand in Mesopotamia.

1276 One of the primary glassmaking cities in the West is Venice, Italy.

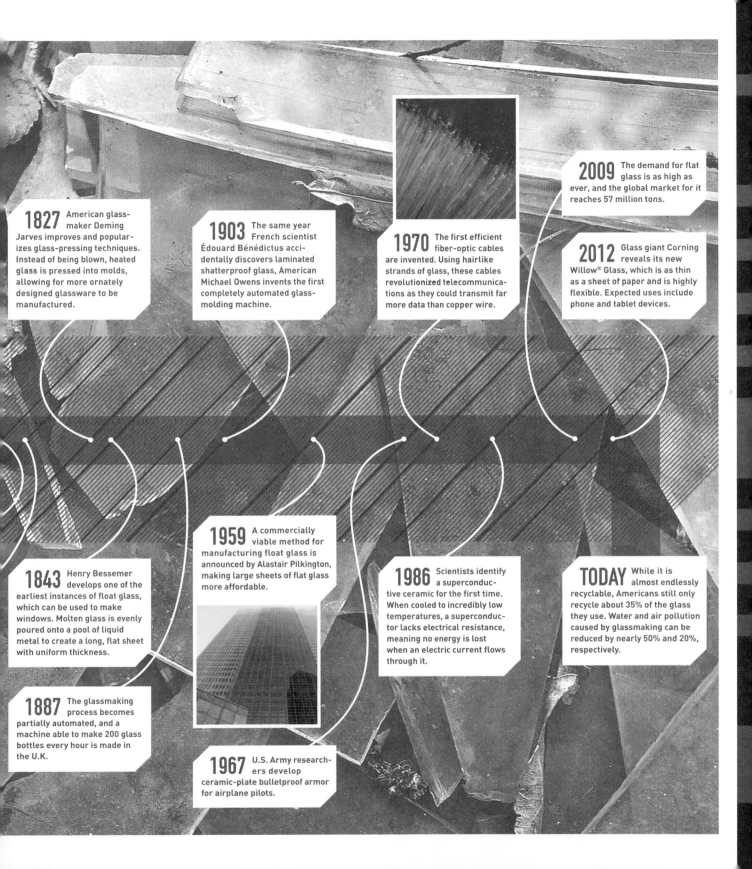

1827 American glass-maker Deming Jarves improves and popularizes glass-pressing techniques. Instead of being blown, heated glass is pressed into molds, allowing for more ornately designed glassware to be manufactured.

1903 The same year French scientist Édouard Bénédictus accidentally discovers laminated shatterproof glass, American Michael Owens invents the first completely automated glass-molding machine.

1970 The first efficient fiber-optic cables are invented. Using hairlike strands of glass, these cables revolutionized telecommunications as they could transmit far more data than copper wire.

2009 The demand for flat glass is as high as ever, and the global market for it reaches 57 million tons.

2012 Glass giant Corning reveals its new Willow® Glass, which is as thin as a sheet of paper and is highly flexible. Expected uses include phone and tablet devices.

1843 Henry Bessemer develops one of the earliest instances of float glass, which can be used to make windows. Molten glass is evenly poured onto a pool of liquid metal to create a long, flat sheet with uniform thickness.

1887 The glassmaking process becomes partially automated, and a machine able to make 200 glass bottles every hour is made in the U.K.

1959 A commercially viable method for manufacturing float glass is announced by Alastair Pilkington, making large sheets of flat glass more affordable.

1967 U.S. Army researchers develop ceramic-plate bulletproof armor for airplane pilots.

1986 Scientists identify a superconductive ceramic for the first time. When cooled to incredibly low temperatures, a superconductor lacks electrical resistance, meaning no energy is lost when an electric current flows through it.

TODAY While it is almost endlessly recyclable, Americans still only recycle about 35% of the glass they use. Water and air pollution caused by glassmaking can be reduced by nearly 50% and 20%, respectively.

For example, countries in the European Union will have to recycle 50 percent of their country's household waste by 2020, according to a waste reduction plan set forth by the E.U. extended producer responsibility laws, or legislation that makes manufacturers and producers responsible for the collection and recycling of their products, are also in effect across the E.U. Some countries have also introduced or raised landfill taxes, incentivizing alternatives like recycling. While the U.S. has avoided far-reaching sustainability or waste management legislation like this, Europe has embraced it.

Out of the top sixteen countries, the U.S. placed fifteenth while the rest of the countries were all from Europe. In addition, five of these countries had rates that were more than double that in the U.S. The highest rate was Switzerland with a whopping 89 percent glass-recycling rate; the U.S. had a measly 33 percent. Many other countries around the world, especially developing countries, don't have high enough numbers to even place.

LOOKING FORWARD

You don't hear environmentalists gripe much about glass, mostly because the material itself is relatively environmentally innocuous. It can be recycled ad infinitum, its component minerals aren't ecologically toxic, and it requires materials that are naturally occurring, like sandstone, sodium bicarbonate, and lime. The market for recycled cullet makes glass waste collections lucrative as well, meaning that it's one of the most highly recycled materials in the world. Not only that, but a glass bottle that's recycled can be remade into a new bottle or container in only about 30 days. If glass packaging were the only waste stream we had to worry about, we'd be in pretty good shape.

But the problem is not glass in itself; it's when glass is mixed with other materials, like metals, plastics, and rubbers to make objects like your favorite perfume bottle, or pair of eye glasses. These hybrids cause a problem because they cannot be easily recycled in the normal glass-recycling systems around the world, as the other materials act as a contaminator (in fact, 25 percent of all glass that is put into local recycling programs is not recycled for this very reason).

At TerraCycle we have set up various collection programs for glass hybrids, such as perfume and cosmetic compacts. Through these programs you can easily, and in many cases for free, send us your glass waste that cannot go into your local municipal recycling stream. We then take these

Collected used glass bottles at a recycling center in London.

materials, shred them, and once the particles are small enough, we separate the glass from the metal and other materials. From there the materials are melted and made into new products.

However, it's not just innovative recycling that will help us curb glass waste. When buying products in glass packaging, try to make choices based on what you can reuse for other purposes. For example, clean out that pasta sauce container and use it to package something else. And especially choose clear glass packaging over colored glass, since clear glass is more desirable to glass recyclers.

WHAT YOU CAN DO

About 3.5 billion compact fluorescent lightbulbs were sold globally in 2003, all of which contained some levels of mercury. If that mercury finds its way into a landfill, there's an enormous risk of it seeping into the ground, where it can pollute drinking water. Correctly recycling lightbulbs is something everyone can do.

Lions Clubs International, Lions Recycle for Sight

LIONS CLUBS INTERNATIONAL is a volunteer network with over 1.35 million members serving 209 countries and geographic areas around the world. As part of their Lions Recycle for Sight initiative, the organization collects old or used eyeglasses, lenses, and frames to recycle and distribute to needy people locally and throughout the world in developing countries.

The Lions Clubs originated in Chicago in 1917 and serves the community in a variety of ways, from scholarships and luncheons to health screenings. It wasn't until Helen Keller served as a guest speaker for the 1925 Lions convention that the Lions Clubs set their sight on sight. Keller asked the organization to become "the knights of the blind in the crusade against darkness." The collections started, and saving sight soon became the group's main mission.

More than 157 million people without access to eye care are affected by poor eyesight. Without corrective lenses, both children and adults are handicapped in education and employment opportunities, not to mention everyday life. Lions set out to fix the issue, collecting millions of used eyeglasses each year. A simple pair of recycled glass lenses can be a new start for millions of underprivileged people.

Used eyeglasses are collected at a variety of community locations such as banks, schools, libraries, and optometrist offices. These collection locations are hosted around the world in the U.S., Spain, South Africa, Italy, France, Canada, and Australia, among others. Volunteers sort and separate the donations, and lensometers determine the prescription of each intact glass lens. During a dispensing mission, trained Lions members and eye care professionals perform vision screenings for needy children and adults in the area. Once their prescription is determined, appropriate glasses are distributed accordingly. All services are free of cost and rely on the efforts of volunteers and donators. While it costs the Lions less than $0.08 U.S. to provide a pair of recycled eyeglasses to one person, to the beneficiary, the impact is priceless.

Recycle A Bulb (recycleabulb.veoliaes.com/home) is a great resource to use, especially for disposing of those pesky mercury-containing compact fluorescent bulbs. After inputting your zip code, Recycle A Bulb's webpage scours its database of over 5,000 drop-off locations around the country for those that are closest to you. Your own town or city may have specific guidelines as well, so it's worth checking out the local government homepage for information. For example, GrowNYC (grownyc.org/cfl), a New York City–based nonprofit, offers New Yorkers a list of drop-off locations in the city. Recycle San Diego (recyclesandiego.org) does the same thing, and has resources for home appliance, electronics, and cell phone recycling as well. Most Home Depot stores and other home improvement stores offer similar take-back programs for burned-out bulbs.

Eyeglasses can be recycled as well. In North America, 4 million of these sight-granting miracles are tossed in the garbage every year. While they might not be the biggest environmental threat, the sight someone could be granted makes it all the sadder (see Lions Clubs International, Lions Recycle for Sight, page 139).

Some multicomponent products contain glass parts that can be difficult to separate after being collected, making recycling a particular challenge. Electronics like computer monitors, old television sets, and some tablet computers have glass or glass-derived screens. Since e-waste is extremely toxic if it hits landfills, donate your old monitors and TVs to a local Goodwill (goodwill.org) instead of throwing them on the side of the road. Goodwill even partners with Dell's Reconnect Program,

The largest glass furnaces produce more than 1 million glass bottles a day.

which recycles or refurbishes computer equipment collected.

The most important point: Be sure to use the glass products you buy for as long as possible before recycling them. If you can find a use for that jelly jar that extends beyond its designed life-cycle (i.e. when you run out of jelly), you can use it in place of a new product you'd otherwise need to buy new.

Anything from a mason jar to an old piece of glass cookware retains its original strength no matter how old it is, so reuse it! The same energy-intensive process was required to make most of these glass objects, so by lengthening their lives you reduce the need to manufacture new products.

Manufacturing line for glass lightbulbs.

GLASS CANDLESTICK HOLDER

Looking for a way to repurpose all of that old, vintage glassware you've been collecting? Then this is the perfect project for you! Painting the insides gives it the look of old milk glass, but they look equally beautiful with the plain glass. For adults.

WHAT YOU NEED

- 4 to 6 small glass items
- Glass paint
- Used newspaper
- E-6000 glue
- Plastic cup for mixing paint
- Detail paintbrush

TIP: TRY A MONOCHROMATIC COLOR SCHEME TO HELP TIE THE DIFFERENT SHAPES TOGETHER.

0

3

1

Start with clean glassware. Pour some paint into a cup and add a very small amount of water to thin it. Mix well. Pour some of this mixture into the glass bottle or vessel and swirl around until bottle is coated. Pour any excess back into the cup of thinned paint. Turn upside down to dry on old newspaper.

2

Arrange the pieces into a column, choosing pieces that fit well together and have enough contact points for the glue to hold well. Begin gluing the pieces together, following the glue manufacturer's instructions for setting.

Continue gluing the pieces together until you've reached the desired height. Once the glue is set, add a candlestick to top off your project.

LIFECYCLE OF A GLASS BOTTLE

3 Next, the gooey, hot glass is poured into a mold where air pressure forms the malleable blob into a familiar bottle shape.

Finally, the most important part: strengthening. The newly formed bottle is sent to an oven called a lehr, where it is repeatedly heated and cooled under strictly controlled conditions to strengthen the glass and remove imperfections.

1 The basic ingredients: silica sand, sodium bicarbonate, limestone, and other additives are collected and prepared for processing.

5 The finished bottle and thousands of its buddies are packaged onto pallets and sent away to beverage producers and factories around the world.

4

2 The concoction is then mixed with water and blasted in a furnace until it melts, reaching temperatures as high as 2,800 degrees Fahrenheit!

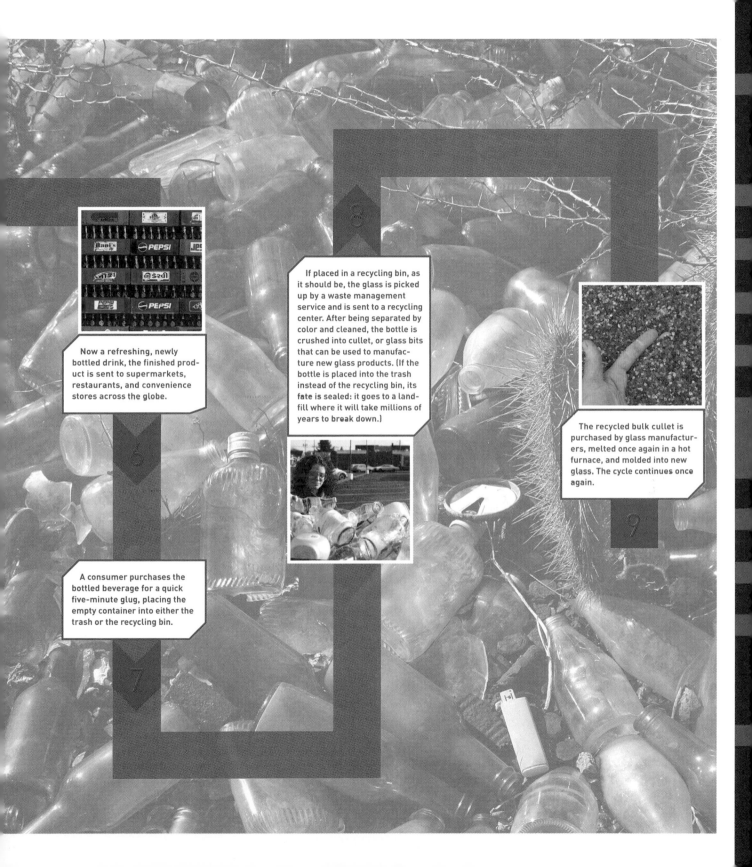

Now a refreshing, newly bottled drink, the finished product is sent to supermarkets, restaurants, and convenience stores across the globe.

If placed in a recycling bin, as it should be, the glass is picked up by a waste management service and is sent to a recycling center. After being separated by color and cleaned, the bottle is crushed into cullet, or glass bits that can be used to manufacture new glass products. (If the bottle is placed into the trash instead of the recycling bin, its fate is sealed: it goes to a landfill where it will take millions of years to break down.)

The recycled bulk cullet is purchased by glass manufacturers, melted once again in a hot furnace, and molded into new glass. The cycle continues once again.

A consumer purchases the bottled beverage for a quick five-minute glug, placing the empty container into either the trash or the recycling bin.

In the U.S., 25% of wood that is cut never enters the commercial flow due to wasteful manufacturing operations.

CHAPTER 6

WOOD

Do you remember the good old days when lush temperate forests and diverse woodland wildlife were found throughout the U.S.? Neither do we, because in the 400 years since colonists first set foot on North America, over 90 percent of the primary forests that once populated our country have been removed. It's estimated that an astounding 3 billion trees are cut down every year worldwide — and some research suggests that number may be as high as 6 billion! While the rate of deforestation has actually slowed from this astronomical number, the vast majority of the old growth forests of the world no longer exist.

Previous spread: Wood waste in landfill; wood pulp piled high (*inset*). // Above: A large cord of wood.

Depending on how deforestation rates fare in the coming years, all of the world's old growth forestland could be removed in only a couple of hundred years. It's a discontinuous cycle across various forest-dense countries; some heavily regulate conservation efforts, while others exponentially increase deforestation rates to maintain enough lumber and timber supply to meet demand.

We live in a world that is still incredibly dependent on wood, hence the continued degradation of rainforests and forestlands throughout the world. The global market for wood products alone is about $250 billion, and that doesn't even include the market for construction and industrial timber.

FIRST USES OF WOOD

We'll begin the story when our ancestors first began to use fire in a controlled manner. Archaeological evidence collected in a South African cave suggests that our not-so-distant relatives may have started using small branches and grass materials for fire about 1 million years ago for cooking.

From then on, it was just a matter of being inventive. The Paleolithic era, the age of stone tools that predates written history, saw an influx of tools and architecture that got increasingly complex. Tools with wooden handles, shelters made out of branches and animal skin, and even weapons for hunting, like spears, could be fashioned together. Wood was sturdy and strong, but could still be broken or cut to the right length with relative ease.

For the next several thousand years, more complex wooden tools and structures would be invented periodically, making the harsh, often nomadic lives of early humans a bit easier to manage. It was around 7000 BCE that inhabitants of northern Europe started using wooden sleds to transport themselves, supplies, and equipment long distances over the icy, snow-blanketed terrain. An early type of wooden plough made land cultivation easier as well, which was getting increasingly necessary as communities of people became more sedentary.

When copper was discovered, ancient "industry" was catalyzed and made more efficient. Woodworking possibilities flourished, and some of the most complex structures of ancient time were crafted. By 4500 BCE, for example, large marine vessels and barges with hollow hulls made of lightweight wood allowed huge amounts of goods and people to be transported long distances over large

Tree poaching is a costly problem in our national parks. In 1996 Washington State disclosed that a total of $1 million in lumber was stolen each month from the state.

bodies of water. The wheel came close to 3000 BCE, and wooden handcarts were close behind.

The secrets of the cork oak tree were even discovered around this time in parts of Asia and the Middle East, where ancient fishermen and women first used cork as fishing tackle.

The world was growing accustomed to wood as a go-to raw material, so much so that the seeds of a global industry for it were already being sewn. The Romans, for instance, established some of the first water-powered sawmills in 250 CE. It was a sign that production was becoming relatively streamlined, as new developments in engineering permeated the civilized world, allowing people to tap into the vast, relatively undisturbed forests that blanketed the land. Extravagant wooden buildings, like the Buddhist temple Horyu in Japan, were testaments to wood's incredible versatility and architectural applications. Built in 607

A commercial lumberyard with timber logs that have been cut down and are ready to be processed.

CE, Horyu's pagoda actually stood as the oldest-standing wooden building in the world until a fire in the late 1800s.

SHORTAGES
As we approach the middle of the first millennium, certain geographic regions began having dangerous shortages of wood and lumber, especially as forests began to get smaller in size as farmlands expanded. For the next several hundred years, Europe faced periodic shortages of wood due to soaring demand. Homes, infrastructure, and ships were getting larger and more intricately designed;

Right: Upcycled coaster or trivet made from used wine corks. // Far right: A half-stripped cork oak tree. // Below: A tree in an urban landscape. // Opposite: The five-story pagoda of Horyu Temple in Ikaruga, Japan.

wood was used to warm people's houses; and a variety of industries required huge amounts of wood to fuel furnaces, smelters, and refineries. While some shortages were likely over-exaggerated by cautious governments that began taking resource management seriously, some regions did indeed see significant wood shortages. It wasn't until forestry started being developed as a field of scientific study in the 1800s that fears of wood shortages would universally decline.

While the demand for wood wasn't entirely mitigated with the onset of the Industrial Revolution, coal generally supplanted it as a fuel source. If anything, coal drove production and manufacturing efficiencies to such a height that wood became even more of an industrial necessity. The growing railroad industry required wood for everything from tracks and bridges, to even the train wagons themselves. Similar engineering even led to the

Every 9 years of a cork oak's 300-year lifespan, its bark is stripped and harvested for industrial use.

The average life expectancy of any tree in an urban or city environment is only 8 years.

first true wooden rollercoaster in 1817, paving the way for more intricate coaster designs. The forest was starting to be utilized to its fullest material potential, even if the environmental costs were still not being fully realized. With such a high dependence on wood, people began to come up with even more ways to ensure that a constant supply of timber, wood, and lumber could be maintained to keep up with demand. The result was the tree farm.

TREE FARMS

A tree farm is essentially just a plot of land—owned privately by a company or group of investors— where trees are grown for the sole purpose of being harvested for commercial use. In the U.S. in 1941, a campaign called the American Tree Farms System was initiated by the National Lumber Manufacturers Association. Interest in the concept was sparked, and soon people across the country were rushing to have their tracts of forestland certified

From the 1950s to today, about one-fifth of earth's forests have been cleared.

FIVE CRAZY THINGS THAT HAVE BEEN MADE OUT OF WOOD

If you thought you knew everything you could use wood for, think again. Here are some of the stranger things we found have been made out of wood, all thanks to some very motivated and talented individuals.

1 Motorcycle: An automotive engineer named Gottlieb Daimler was known in the mid- to late 1800s for his complex wooden mechanical designs, even one of the first motorcycles—made almost entirely out of wood! In similar spirit, a Hungarian man named Istvan Puskas made a wooden motorcycle himself at his home in 2014, complete with wooden handlebars, seats, chassis, and wheels.

2 Lightbulbs: You can actually buy your very own, very cool wooden lightbulbs online at suck.uk.com. A mix of art and function, they were designed by Barend Hemmes, and while they may not be the most convenient bulbs to replace, they sure look beautiful.

3 123-Foot Building: There's a good reason skyscrapers are made out of steel and not wood, but a 123-foot-tall church in Russia made completely out of wood has been standing for more than 150

years without a problem. Kizhi Pogost is the Russian Orthodox Church in question. The church is so tall that, since it was built, it remains the tallest wooden building on the planet.

4 Computer: Designer Marlies Romberg rejects using unsustainable materials in her work. That's why the "Dear Diary 1.0" is actually a functional computer made mostly out of wood. Everything from the monitor to the keyboard and even the mouse is made out of perfectly crafted wood, right down to the numbering on the keyboard keys.

5 An Entire House: By "an entire house" we mean an entire house. An artist from Venice named Livio De Marchi has turned his home into a wood museum, because just about every single thing within it is made of wood. From the light fixtures, tables, chairs, and tableware, to the teddy bears, handbags, and books on the shelves, every corner of the house is covered by pieces made by De Marchi. Even the "tablecloths" covering various surfaces and his piano are artfully crafted pieces of wood.

About half of the country's hardwood is made into pallets or crates that are thrown away after just one use.

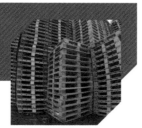

Above: Daimler's first motorcycle prototype. // Left: A mountainous stack of wooden pallets.

The rate of trees lost globally each year is 10 times greater than the number of trees gained during regrowth. This number adds up to an astonishing 40 million acres of forest destruction each year.

Slash-and-burn cultivation, to clear the rainforest to plant maize seedlings, in the Peruvian Amazon.

as "tree farms." In 1941 there were 120,000 acres of tree farms; in 1943 there were more than 7 million; and 17 million by 1949. Tree farms allowed industry leaders to maintain a front of environmental stewardship and "conservation" efforts, while really just managing the demand for wood and wood products. The forest was enduring a hostile takeover of the human kind, all in the name of industry, capital, and more important, money.

The Christmas tree industry is a good example of the state of tree farming today. At U.S. tree farms today, about 400 million evergreen conifers are being grown specifically for the Christmas season. With such a high demand for Christmas trees (and

on regular tree farms, for timber and lumber in general), efficiency is a top priority. Farms can contain millions of trees, and are often spread across thousands of acres of land. Most tree seeds are planted with machines that can plant entire rows at a time. After planting, it can take upward of ten years for a tree to grow to the required height. When they are ready to be cut down, dozens of trees are transported together to a preparation area to await shipping. Once packed onto a truck, they are shipped across the country to be sold.

Today there are some certification programs to ensure forestlands are being maintained as sustainably as possible. The American Tree Farm

System has evolved somewhat, requiring certified foresters to follow strict sustainability guidelines in order to receive an ATFS Certification. Some states also offer certifications for in-state forest owners. While it does not prevent the wholesale deforestation of our old growth forestlands, it does bring accountability back to those who capitalize on them.

A REPLACEMENT FOR WOOD

Lumber, or wood that's used primarily in construction applications, didn't really have any viable replacements or alternatives until the late twentieth century. In 1973, a man named Irvin Vincent developed for his company, the N.E.W. Plastics Corp., the first lumber made entirely from plastic. Like TerraCycle's own plastic lumber made from recycled plastic packaging (like drink pouches), Vincent's plastic lumber was made from recycled plastic, specifically the high-density polyethylene that a typical milk jug is made from. While it might only mitigate a small portion of the wood material we continue to take directly from forestlands, it certainly does help that it diverts plastic packaging waste from landfills while also preventing virgin wood from being harvested.

But there's clearly not enough recycled plastic lumber out there to completely mitigate the amount of lumber we consume on a regular basis. In 2005 for instance, people across the world consumed 14 billion cubic feet of sawed wood alone. The good news is that this is actually 1.7 billion less than 1990. The decrease is probably due to better recycling practices, along with some help from the recycled plastic lumber industry. Still, it's not like we're becoming a species of tree-hugging environmentalists; from 2000 to 2010, humans cut down an average 12.8 million acres of forestland each year.

FORESTS DO IMPORTANT WORK

Our old growth forests are important to forest critters and human beings alike—and some research suggests that they absorb more carbon dioxide than tree farms. Because old growth consists of trees of varying age, the canopy is

Left: Rows of poplars at a tree farm, which are being grown to become paper. // Right: A new home being built with wood framing, roof, trusses, supports, and wall.

WINE CORK STOPPER

Trying to figure out how to save that leftover wine? Make a reusable wine stopper out of a cork and a doorknob. Not only will you save the wine, but you also save the environment from trash. For adults.

WHAT YOU NEED

- Wine cork
- Doorknob/handle
- Screwdriver (optional)
- Hacksaw (optional)
- Polyurethane glue
- Hobby knife

1

Take apart your doorknob and remove any locking mechanisms or other parts of the unit that are non-essential — basically anything other than the knob itself. You may have to use the screwdriver and hacksaw to remove some parts.

2

Apply a small amount of glue to the cork, and secure it inside the open end of the doorknob.

WOOD TIMELINE

PALEOLITHIC ERA
Early Stone Age human beings discover wood and many of its applications, and things like weapons, simple furniture, and better tools are produced.

1750 Ancient Egyptians popularize a method for making plywood out of alternating layers of wood, gluing them together into a board with substances like hot cartilage and bone. The plywood was used for basic structures and carts.

7000 BCE People in northern Europe use wooden sleds to drag and move people and goods across long tracts of ice in the cold, snowy climate.

5000 Durable tools made out of materials like copper allow wood to be worked with in more complex ways allowing more end uses of the wood being worked.

250 CE In what is today Turkey, the Romans construct one of the first-known sawmills using water power.

1000 One of the first wooden printing presses is invented in Asia.

4500 Large, hollow wooden barges start cropping up for long-distance transportation over water.

6000 The first plows, made out of wood and pulled by a single worker, are invented.

3000 The wheel is invented! As hand-carts and other wheeled objects start being made, cork from cork oak is used as tackle for fishing lines in parts of Asia and the Middle East.

607 The longest-standing wooden building, the pagoda of the Horyu Temple in Japan, was built this year. Controversy still plagues the temple, however, as a fire destroyed much of it in the 1800s, leading many to instead call it a reconstruction of the original.

1333 The longest-known wooden bridge in Europe is constructed in Switzerland, called the Kapell-brücke, or Chapel Bridge. A fire in 1993 destroyed most of the bridge, but it was subsequently rebuilt and is still used today.

1800 Railroads use wood in a variety of ways: fuel and the construction of train wagons, bridges, and infrastructure.

1848 Wood becomes a viable material for papermaking after the wood-pulping machine is invented, opening up the forests to paper manufacturers for the first time.

1990 Bamboo starts to increase in popularity in the hardwood floor market, as it grows exceptionally quickly and can be collected without damaging the plant itself.

2010 The first decade of the new millennium saw an average 12.8 million acres of forest lost around the world every single year.

1817 The first wooden rollercoaster is built in France. Known as the "Russes a Belleville," the idea would soon lead to more intricate tracks, larger designs, and multiple-car designs for more people.

1916 An early plastic-composite alternative for wood is used to manufacture a type of gearshift for Rolls-Royce, one of the first times a plastic and wood composite material is used in a consumer product.

1973 The first plastic lumber, made out of recycled high-density polyethylene plastic, is invented by plastic industrialist Irvin Vincent.

2005 Approximately 14.8 million cubic feet of sawed wood are consumed globally, about 50 million less than in 1990. This is likely due to greater recycling efforts and the increased use of plastic composite alternatives to wood.

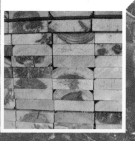

TODAY We're cutting down billions of trees every year to sustain our current consumption of wood and its products. In the U.S., the average person goes through approximately seven trees' worth of wood products every year. If all of the wood products, including paper, that end up trashed by Americans every year were instead used for heating, 50 million houses could be heated for the next 20 years.

FOUR SUSTAINABLE ALTERNATIVES TO WOOD

Wood is technically a renewable resource because we can replant trees, but that doesn't mean deforestation isn't still a huge environmental crisis. Thankfully there are plenty of materials out there that have similar properties to wood, or can at least emulate it in certain ways.

1 Bamboo: Actually a type of grass, bamboo is one of the most useful plants humans have ever discovered. It grows exceptionally fast, can be as strong as many types of wood, and resists moisture. It's also easy to grow and harvest, which makes it a cheap crop to produce.

2 Recycled Plastic: Both composite and pure recycled plastic lumber are great alternatives as they use existing plastic waste and limit the need for virgin lumber. Composites can be made by combining wood leftovers and plastic, and plastic lumber is usually made with 100% recycled plastic like HDPE.

3 Hemp: An incredibly versatile plant, hemp can be a substitution for wood in certain applications. Hemp fiberboard is stronger than wood, and could possibly even replace plywood down the road. It grows quickly and efficiently, too: one acre of hemp creates more usable material than one acre of trees.

4 Newspaper: A Dutch designer named Mieke Meijer crafted a beautiful wood alternative completely out of used newspapers. The lines of text and layers of paper even look like authentic wood grain when cut. The best part is that it's functional, and can be sanded or cut. Other companies actively manufacture fiberboard made out of, among other fibers, recycled newspaper.

uneven. This means that when a large tree finally falls to the forest floor, younger trees below are exposed to the sunlight, absorbing more carbon dioxide. Removing old growth to start a tree farm in fact releases carbon dioxide, and it can take as long as 20 years before the planted trees grow enough to absorb meaningful levels of the greenhouse gas.

There is a reason why the Amazon rainforest is also known as "the Lungs of the Earth." Trees and other plants absorb large amounts of carbon dioxide from our atmosphere, preventing it from accumulating in the atmosphere. When carbon dioxide and other greenhouse gases accumulate, they trap heat from the sun within the earth's atmosphere. Trees and forests essentially protect the planet in this way, keeping it cooler while helping prevent dramatic shifts in climate.

Our forests should be protected and maintained, yet we continue to disregard many of the factors that lead to their destruction. For instance, if you purchase a wood product, you are increasing the demand for logging and deforestation. Some

Opposite: Bamboo // Left: Lumberjack cutting a tree, which will be sent to a mill to be processed into lumber.

products, like hardwood floors made from exotic tropical lumber, can even drive demand for illegal logging in dwindling rainforests. Even simply throwing wood away instead of recycling is damaging—we could heat 50 million homes for 20 years straight with the amount of wood thrown away annually in the U.S.

WOOD TODAY

Although wood is a renewable resource, there are environmental issues surrounding its harvesting. Our need for wood sometimes stands in opposition to our need for trees. The biggest threats are logging and deforestation, which are in some ways the two heads of one big, tree-eating monster.

The same amount of carbon a car emits driving 26,000 miles can be consumed by just one tree.

DEFORESTATION AND LOGGING

Forests cover 31 percent of land on our planet, and house 70 percent of the world's land animals and plants. We lose forests at a rate of about 48 football fields per minute. Deforestation poses a huge threat to the environment, contributing to everything from the desecration of the land to the pollution of the air. Some of the world's most biologically diverse forests are in danger, including the Amazon and the Congo Basin.

There are a number of different causes of deforestation. However, we're going to focus on the illegal logging and fuelwood harvesting industries, as both directly connect our need for wood with the destruction of the earth's natural resources. About 40 percent of the world's population still relies on fuelwood or charcoal as their primary source of energy for essentials like cooking and heating. These numbers tend to be high in areas around rainforests and large forests, and fuel harvesting remains an important factor in their deforestation. For instance, in the late 1990s, a refugee camp was set up in eastern Congo and relied on wood from the Virunga National Park as its main source of energy and building materials. In just a few months, more than 20,000 acres of park had been cleared!

Subtropical rainforest and mountains in Springbrook National Park in Queensland, Australia.

Deforestation in dry climates can also contribute to desertification, or when drylands slowly transform and degrade into arid tracts of desert. Some of the poorest areas of the world in continents like Africa and Asia are subjected to increased rates of desertification.

One of the main problems with the logging industry (besides the obvious loss of trees) is the pollution that the actual act of logging produces. Logging roads and trucks discharge sediments and other pollutants into clean water sources, polluting the water and threatening the plants, animals, and humans that depend on it to survive.

Though legal logging is a huge issue to the environment, illegal logging may be an even bigger threat. The logging industry has to follow certain legal restrictions, including respecting protected areas and not cutting more than their authorized quota. Illegal logging follows no such codes and threatens to destroy some of the world's most important forests. In some areas of the world, illegal logging is more common than the legal variety. In fact, in the late 1990s, it was estimated that 80 percent of all logging in Brazil was illegal. Illegal logging decreases the value of timber and hurts law-abiding timber companies. Illegal logging also poses a threat to poor communities near large forests; they are often taken advantage of by these shady businesses.

The effects of deforestation are devastating. Remember all of those plants and animals that we talked about that make their homes in forests? Well, once those forests are destroyed, those species either need to find a new home or they could be in danger of dying out. They aren't the only ones at risk, though. Trees absorb carbon dioxide and other harmful greenhouse gases, while also providing coverage for the damp soil underneath

Of all the renewable energy consumed globally, nearly a third of it is wood fuel used by private households for cooking and heating.

Weather-worn wooden planks.

THREE WAYS TO MAKE SURE YOUR WOOD PRODUCTS ARE ECO-FRIENDLY

Just because it's made of wood doesn't mean it was produced sustainably or in a socially responsible way. If you want to start being a conscious consumer, these are a few ways to help.

1 Use Reclaimed Wood: Instead of buying fresh-sawed wood, try using reclaimed wood. Lumber that's labeled reclaimed means that it was once used or was found at the bottom of a lake or in old orchard fields. It's one of the best forms of reuse, and can come with some cool historical surprises. For example, some might have been cut pre–World War II, a time when stronger, older trees were cut to get lumber. You'll be integrating a bit of sustainability and history directly into your home!

2 Check for Certification Labels: If you notice a label saying that a wood product is certified by an organization like the Forest Stewardship Council (us.fsc.org) or the Rainforest Alliance (rainforest-alliance.org), you can rest assured knowing that the wood was collected as sustainably as possible. These certifications are important to go by, as deforestation is still a far more relevant issue than most realize.

Being certified by organizations like these is an honor that can greatly benefit product companies, but requires strict guidelines to be met. For example, the Forest Stewardship Council requires that the indigenous population of a region be respected when managing forestlands, and using pesticides or genetically modified trees is prohibited.

3 Avoid Tropical Species: Hardwood flooring is often made using certain tropical species of trees. It's great for the look of your home, but not so great for the old growth in the rainforests the trees came from. Jatoba, for instance, is a species often used to make what's known as Brazilian cherry hardwood flooring. Demand for the hardwood is so high that it even catalyzes illegal deforestation in the Amazon. Tropical trees like this are often found in old growth, or forest area that has existed undisturbed for many centuries. It should also be noted that just because a tropical wood is certified by the Forest Stewardship Council doesn't mean that the wood wasn't sourced from old growth. The best thing you can do is avoid these varieties of wood altogether.

them. So guess what happens when these trees are cut down? There's no longer anything to absorb these gases for us, and once they're cut or burned they become carbon sources. In fact, deforestation represents around 15 percent of global greenhouse gas emissions. That damp soil that relied on the trees to cover it is also out of luck. Without

the trees to protect it, it can dry out, changing the entire ecosystem. Soil erosion is another issue. When the trees are destroyed, there's nothing to anchor fertile soil, which can lead to it being swept into nearby rivers. The crops that are sometimes planted in the tree's wake (forests are often destroyed to make room for agriculture)

> For in the true nature of things, if we rightly consider, every green tree is far more glorious than if it were made of gold and silver.
> — Martin Luther

A far too common image of deforestation. Here the trees are being cut for lumber.

often can't act as anchors for the soil, meaning that farmers have to abandon the area to start this entire cycle somewhere else.

Around 24.7 million acres of tree farms already exist worldwide, and about 2.5 million acres of land are converted to farms each year. But these tree farms are not actual forests, because there's no diversity in the type of tree that's being planted. These farms are monocultures, meaning that the same type of tree is being planted over and over again. They also require a lot of human involvement, including a heavy use of pesticides. And, because these farms are typically built in developing countries, they are taking land away from indigenous people without offering them anything in return.

LOOKING FORWARD

At TerraCycle we have come to the issue of wood waste by creating wood alternatives, such as recycling plastic packaging waste into plastic lumber that could replace natural lumber, limiting the need to cut down more trees. Plastic lumber is not only a great substitute for wood, it is made from waste, is significantly more durable than normal wood, can come in any color and size, resists water damage, and is insect and mold proof.

There are countless other products that rely on wood to manufacture too, like the wine barrels that we have upcycled into rain barrels and rotary

One reason wood consumption has increased is because the average size of homes has increased significantly, with floor space per person more than doubling in new homes between 1949 and 1993.

Most new-construction houses are made out of wood, especially pine.

composters. The benefits of this are that the wood product (the wine barrel, which was typically used only once before being discarded by the wine maker) has an extended lifecycle of use, allowing us to get the most out of the trees that were cut down to produce it.

As with all waste streams, the best way to decrease wood waste is to use less wood. And when wood is needed, use reclaimed wood or wood alternatives.

WHAT OTHERS ARE DOING

The Alliance for Green Heat (forgreenheat.org) is an organization that provides resources for in-need individuals on how to find free firewood to heat their homes. The organization hosts annual design challenges hoping to inspire innovation and the development of more efficient, improved wood stoves. On a global level, the nonprofit Potential Energy (potentialenergy.org) builds more efficient wood-burning stoves in developing nations, saving impoverished people money while lessening the amount of wood needed to burn.

The Rainforest Alliance (rainforest-alliance.org) is another nonprofit hoping to reduce defor-estation in tropical regions, especially the Amazon Rainforest in South America. The Alliance provides students and teachers with educational lesson plans to teach about forest conservation, as well as an Adopt-A-Rainforest program that allows orga-nizations and schools to help contribute funding to smaller conservation efforts and organizations

Forest Stewardship Council (FSC)

DEEP WITHIN THE MORE UNREGULATED PARTS OF THE WORLD, illegal logging and bad forest management practices destroy some of the oldest, most diverse forestlands on the planet. Unfortunately for consumers, finding out which wood products are made safely, sustainably, and legally can be a challenge. The Forest Stewardship Council (FSC) wants to eliminate that challenge, while pushing forest managers into becoming stewards of the environment instead of ravagers of it.

The nonprofit FSC came to fruition in the early 1990s after efforts to limit global deforestation failed at the 1992 Earth Summit. The first official FSC General Assembly finally met in 1993, where various environmentalists, entrepreneurs, companies, and social activists met to collaborate on how to end bad forest management practices that led to deforestation and the destruction of precious, and extremely diverse, old growth forests. Since then, the FSC has grown into a massive international organization, with offices in more than 80 different countries—or, as the FSC says of itself, "wherever forests are present."

The primary form of forest protection comes in the form of a highly respected certification system. There are two forms of certification: the Forest Management certification assures that wood collected in the certified forest was grown and harvested responsibly, and that the surrounding indigenous populations, labor force, and environment (among many other criteria) are protected.

The Chain-of-Custody certification ensures that wood harvested sustainably and responsibly maintains its environmental stewardship all the way to the consumer. Lumber might be harvested and processed, then shipped to a manufacturer. In order to maintain the FSC label, that next company must also become Chain-of-Custody certified. This is why it is important to look not only for the Forest Management label on your favorite wood products but the Chain-of-Custody certification as well.

There are 10 official Principles and 57 Criteria that define what an FSC-certified forest is. Owners of certified forestland must respect local workers and indigenous populations, conserve water and expended resources, use forest materials efficiently and without waste, draft detailed plans on how forests will be managed, and constantly assess existing plans and systems currently in place.

The benefit of this certification system is that it has a place in product marketing, as having an FSC-certified label on a product is a lucrative marketing tool for manufacturers.

A cut log containing the logo of the Forest Stewardship Council, indicating it was harvested responsibly.

Clockwise from top left: A light sconce in a TerraCycle meeting room made from pieces of an old wooden wine barrel. // A fake deer trophy made from scrap lumber by TerraCycle designers. // TerraCycle upcycled pens made from old twigs.

WINDOW PICTURE FRAME

Construction materials are often difficult to recycle, but they still hold a lot of character and charm. Find a salvaged window and you're on your way to completing this picture-perfect project. Ideally you should have the same number of photos as panes in the window you use. Of course you can leave some panes open for adding photos later! For adults.

WHAT YOU NEED

- Wooden paned window
- Photos larger than the windowpanes
- 2 screw eyes
- Picture hanging wire
- Glue dots or double-sided tape
- Ruler
- Pen
- Scissors
- Wire cutters

Measure the size of each windowpane.

Use the window measurement to measure and mark that size on your photo. Cut along your marked lines.

TIP: YOU CAN USE AN EXTRA-LARGE PHOTO TO FRAME INSIDE THE WINDOW. PRINT YOUR PHOTO TO THE SIZE OF THE WINDOW.

Place glue dots on the four corners of your photo and place inside the windowpane.

Continue to cut and place your photos inside the window until all of the panes are filled.

Measure 3 inches from the top along both edges of your window frame. Then, screw in your eye hooks into the marked holes.

Thread your wire through the eye hooks so that the wire spans across the width of your window. Twist the ends of the wire back around the wire strand making sure that it is securely fastened.

in countries with rainforests in need of protecting. And, similar to the Forest Stewardship Council, the Rainforest Alliance operates a certification program for companies that use rainforest-sourced wood or land to produce their products. The certification is one layer of assurance that a product donning the Rainforest Alliance label was manufactured in a socially responsible way.

WHAT YOU CAN DO

Your ability to ease the pressure we put on forestlands is only limited by your willingness to make a few small changes in your life. For one, reuse wood scraps as often as you can manage. Reclaimed wood, or wood that was salvaged from old buildings and other projects, is a great way to reuse instead of buying new. Shavings, dust, and chips can be beneficial to homemade compost, while leftover timber or lumber from a DIY or renovation project can be resold, even donated. Habitat for Humanity (habitat.org) accepts construction material donations in the U.S. and Canada; you just have to type in your zip code and state or province to find out where you can bring the supplies.

When possible, replacing sawn wood with 100 percent recycled plastic lumber can also help reduce the pressure on the market for wood construction products. Recycled plastic lumber helps reduce plastic waste while replacing virgin timber. It's a great alternative on a material level, too, utilizing all of the durability and flame-resistant traits of plastic while still being relatively eco-friendly. The point is not to start shifting our dependence away from wood and toward plastic, but to use the waste streams that are floating around us to our advantage. If we can

CONTINUED ON PAGE 170 →

About 76% of the world's timber is consumed by only about 20% of the global population.

LIFECYCLE OF A TABLE

1 We start our journey with trees freshly cut from a forest. These logs are transported to a sawmill facility.

2 The logs are soaked in water for about 20 minutes to wash off mud and to soften the wood.

3 The logs then go through the debarker, and then, depending on their size, they go through different saws to be cut into various sizes and pieces. Some pieces go through another saw and are cut again.

4 These pieces are smoothed and the edges are trimmed off, and are finally sorted into different bins depending on their size.

5 Once the pieces are sorted, the wood is dried and stacked to be shipped to manufacturers.

6 Table manufacturers buy parts pre-made from a supplier.

7 The parts arrive already sanded, and are sanded again to prepare them for staining.

8 Workers inspect the wood parts with fluorescent lights to check for any flaws that might show up when they stain the wood.

Then they spray the table with sealant to protect the staining and to protect the table from humidity. The sealant is sanded to prepare the table for a coat of clear lacquer. It protects the wood from scratches and it gives it a nice shine. Then the table is placed in an oven to cure the lacquer.

13

12

Once all the parts have passed inspection, assembly of the table begins.

The factory then adds the table legs depending on customer preference.

After the table is checked, it moves to the finishing department where it is stained. Workers then whip off the excess stain and there is another inspection. If they didn't catch any flaws before, they will clearly see the flaws now. Every imperfection is sanded down.

9

14

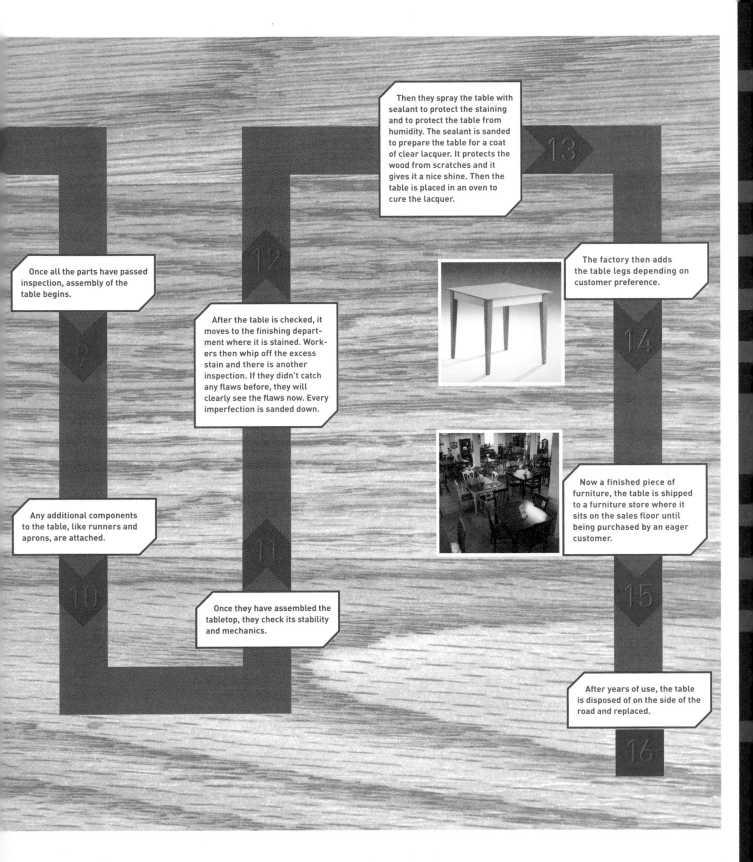

Any additional components to the table, like runners and aprons, are attached.

Now a finished piece of furniture, the table is shipped to a furniture store where it sits on the sales floor until being purchased by an eager customer.

11

10

Once they have assembled the tabletop, they check its stability and mechanics.

15

After years of use, the table is disposed of on the side of the road and replaced.

16

WINE CORK MEMOBOARD

Uncork your creativity and reuse your wine cork collection to create your own personalized memoboard. Wine corks are the perfect material for holding pushpins and a great way to preserve some of your favorite mementos. For adults.

WHAT YOU NEED

- 75 to 100 wine corks
- 11 x 14-inch picture frame
- Cardboard (needs to match or be cut to the size of the outside measurements of your picture frame)
- Pen
- Glue gun
- Hobby knife
- Cutting mat

0

1

Collect your wine corks. Select corks that are approximately the same size.

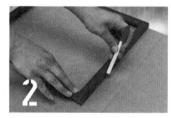

2

Remove the glass and back from your picture frame. Lay the frame on top of the piece of cardboard. Trace around the outside edge.

TIP: YOU CAN SCALE UP THIS PROJECT BY USING A LARGER PICTURE FRAME AND EVEN MORE WINE CORKS!

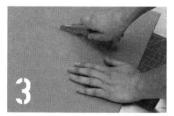

3

Cut the cardboard along the traced line. If there is picture-hanging hardware on the back of your frame, cut around the area. The leftover glass can be recycled!

4

Hot glue the cardboard onto the back of the picture frame.

5 Begin to lay out your wine corks. Create a zigzag pattern by lining up the end of one cork, perpendicular to the side end of the neighboring cork. Gaps around edges are okay and will be filled in later.

6 Continue to lay out your corks until your frame is filled. Glue down each cork with hot glue.

7 Place a wine cork on an area with a gap and mark the size on the cork.

8 Cut along the marked line carefully using the hobby knife and cutting mat. Glue into place.

9 Continue to fill in the gaps with pieces of wine corks until the frame is completely covered.

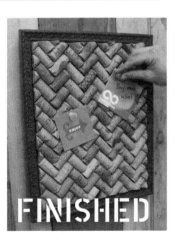

FINISHED

Around the world more than 2 billion people still depend on energy from wood to use for cooking or in heating of homes.

Close-up of a wood-burning stove.

reduce the amount of milk jugs and plastic bottles floating in our rivers, all while building playgrounds for children out of recycled plastic lumber, why wouldn't we do it?

These are decisions to make that do not solve our dependence on wood entirely, or even mitigate the effects of deforestation altogether. They are incremental steps that put us on the path toward a more sustainable future. Just because we can plant new trees does not make deforestation a nonissue, or mean that tree farms are the ultimate solutions. These are merely bandages placed over an unsustainable system that depletes resources and puts undue pressure on the environment, and we are directly responsible for it.

If you're lucky enough to still have trees in your backyard, take a moment to go out and appreciate them. Take a second to absorb just how lucky we are to be able to witness these majestic natural structures grow, some of which are hundreds of years old. We should be protecting those trees with all the effort we can muster, and the first step toward accomplishing that is by appreciating the ones that are standing right in our own backyards.

WHAT WE CAN LEARN FROM EASTER ISLAND

If you want a good picture of where we might be headed, all it takes is to look at a picture of a small Polynesian island in the Pacific Ocean called Easter Island. A small civilization once inhabited the island, settling there around 1200 CE. Easter Island is known for the massive stone statues, likely built by the Polynesians, that pepper the island, some weighing more than 70 tons. What Easter Island is also known for is a complete and utter lack of trees.

Even though it's a small patch of land about the size of Washington, D.C., it's been estimated that Easter Island was once home to 16 million trees. Back in 1200 CE, it was likely a bustling ecosystem of wildlife and humans living in relative harmony with one another. But of course, as populations expand so too does the need for more raw materials. By the year 1400, most of the island was completely devoid of forest or plant life. Millions of trees, plants, and even several species of birds simply disappeared from the island, never to be seen again.

The reason for Easter Island's lack of plant life and forestland is likely due to a mix of issues that plagued the Polynesians. Such a small land mass couldn't sustain a growing population forever, and the growing need for wood likely led to faster-paced deforestation. Then came the rats. New research from the University of Hawaii suggests that the island was probably overrun by rats from European trade vessels. These rats provided a good source of food for the island's inhabitants, but also helped increase the rate of deforestation as the rats began eating away at the tree roots. This combined with a growing population was an ecological recipe for disaster.

Today, Easter Island is a barren landscape of giant stone statues and a treeless horizon. It is an eerie reminder that we should be protecting our natural resources, not recklessly and unsustainably destroying them.

Left: Easter Island statues. // Opposite: Cut lumber.

What they were thinking was that big pieces of lumber like this should be used to make tables or chairs or to repair a house or make window frames; wood like this was hard to find. But now they were cutting it into kindling to be burned in stoves, a sad ending for good wood like this. They could see a comparison with their own lives, and this was a saddening thought.

—Xiao Hong, *Selected Stories of Xiao Hong*

PALLET TABLE

Pallets are perfect for that rustic look and, better yet, they are usually free! There are lots of options for legs, so choose something that goes with your decor. If you are looking for extra durability, add a coat or two of furniture wax when finished. For ages 16 and up.

WHAT YOU NEED

- Pallet
- 12 wood screws
- 4 salvaged table legs
- ¼- to ⅜-inch-thick glass, cut to size of pallet top
- Wood stain
- Spray paint
- Screwdriver or drill
- 60-80 grit sandpaper
- Palm sander or sanding block
- Paint or stain brush

1 Begin by sanding the entire pallet, to remove any debris and splinters. It doesn't need to be perfectly smooth; a little imperfection is part of its charm. Wipe it down afterward to remove the sanding dust.

2 Stain or paint your pallet, if desired, or leave it natural. If you choose to paint or stain, be certain that you cover all of it, including underneath for a more professional look. (Dry time depends on the stain or paint you use; check the back of the product's packaging.)

TIP: ANOTHER OPTION FOR TABLE LEGS WOULD BE TO USE LARGE CASTER WHEELS THAT CAN BE FOUND AT MOST HOME IMPROVEMENT STORES.

Remove the legs from an old table to repurpose them for the new table.

Finish the table legs however you like; for example, apply a finish such as spray paint or stain to give the legs some flair.

Attach the legs by turning your pallet upside down and attaching your legs to the four corners. Attachment methods will vary depending on the type of legs.

Turn your new upcycled pallet table over, place the glass on top, and you're finished. Find the perfect spot for your new pallet table and enjoy!

FINISHED

Every decently made object, from a house to a lamppost to a bridge, spoon, or egg cup, is not just a piece of "stuff" but a physical embodiment of human energy, testimony to the magical ability of our species to take raw materials and turn them into things of use, value, and beauty.

— KEVIN McCLOUD, DESIGNER

Approximately 7 gallons of oil are required to produce one rubber tire. Five gallons are used to extract the raw materials used to form synthetic rubber, and the other two supply the energy for the manufacturing process.

CHAPTER 7

RUBBER

Twenty-three billion pounds. That's how much rubber we produce globally every year, whether it's for new bike tubes, a rubber mouth guard, or the erasers on your child's number 2 pencils. It helps produce nearly 160 billion protective rubber gloves and 1 billion car tires every year around the world, products that make our lives immeasurably safer and more efficient. A lot of rubber comes naturally from certain varieties of plants and trees, so some of it can even be considered a renewable resource. Besides, it's what bouncy balls are made with.

Take the 100 billion gloves thrown away annually, or the 27 million scrap tires that end up in U.S. landfills every year. Because synthetic rubber products will often never biodegrade much of the rubber waste stream is still laying around the planet.

Rubber is the main component in many of our most common products. You might find it on the floor padding of your dining room chairs, in the soles of your shoes, protecting you in impact-absorbing sports equipment, or insulating some wiring behind your wall. The versatility of it as a raw material has made our lives incredibly simpler, even if the rubber as we know it today wasn't even introduced to the western world until the eighteenth century.

BOUNCY BEGINNINGS

If you were a member of the Olmec civilization around 1400 BCE, you may have been forced to play a game that can only be described as a cross between sport and human sacrifice. Known by ancient Mesoamericans as ōllamaliztli, this soccerlike game required players to keep a rubber ball aloft using their hips. These games were typically followed by displays of human sacrifice. Let's not focus on the game itself, though. Let's focus on the ball. The ball is maybe our earliest example of a product made out of rubber. Because of the abundance of Para rubber trees (called *Hevea*

Previous spread; A pile of used tires; oil rig *(inset)*. // Above: A common stone carving of a head from the Olmecs, who were the ancestors of the Aztecs. // Opposite: The molds used to manufacture latex gloves.

brasiliensis) growing in the rainforest, rubber was a vital part of Mesoamerican culture. The Aztecs even referred to their ancestors, the Olmecs, as the "rubber people." Even though Mesoamericans had been using rubber for hundreds of years, the material didn't exist in Europe. Imagine the historian Padre d'Anghieria's surprise when, during a visit to the area in 1525, he saw Mexicans playing with an elastic, bouncy ball.

So the Europeans were a little late to the rubber party. In 1735, a French explorer named Charles-Marie de la Condamine journeyed to South America and sent a sample of rubber back to Europe, along with a letter describing possible uses and means of production. This was a groundbreaking discovery for the Europeans, who until

Before British engineer Edward Nairne accidentally invented erasers in the mid-nineteenth century, most people used bread crumbs to rub out pencil marks.

A NEW RUBBER GLOVE

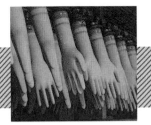

Disposable rubber gloves are a necessary part of our lives whether we like it or not. They protect us from a multitude of diseases, bacteria, and other pathogens, allowing medical personnel to do their jobs and food to be prepared without contamination or spreading disease. We use about 200 billion disposable gloves every year around the world, and even though that translates to a lot of one-use gloves ending up in the trash, we have few alternatives capable of keeping us so well protected.

Of all the varieties of disposable gloves out there, latex used to be the most common. They're strong, resistant to puncturing, and are very elastic so they fit just about any hand size. But the one major drawback is that many people are allergic to latex, or more specifically, latex proteins. Three million people have latex allergies in the U.S. alone.

This concern is why many industries have been shifting away from latex and toward a material called nitrile rubber. Nitrile gloves are made with a synthetic plastic, so there are no latex allergy concerns. These gloves are a bit less elastic than latex ones, but they are even more resistant to chemicals and being punctured. At TerraCycle, we've even partnered with glove and cleaning-product manufacturer Kimberly-Clark Professional to recycle these types of gloves. This means we are able to enjoy the safety and protection benefits, without making the environment suffer in return.

To get a better sense of how necessary disposable rubber gloves are, here are a few ways they protect you, your family, your food, and other people every single day.

Gardening: Fertilizer, pesticides, even compost can all contain dangerous things you don't want to come into contact with. Many fertilizers contain compounds like sulfur and lime, ammonium sulfate, phosphoric acid, and other chemicals that provide nutrients to soil or plants, but can burn your eyes and skin (even lungs if inhaled). Compost is often made with uneaten food waste, so it may contain salmonella and E. coli. As a first line of defense, wearing rubber gloves can drastically reduce the chance that you'll be carrying any of these dangerous pathogens and materials around with you.

Medicine: Healthcare workers already expose themselves to diseases that put them at constant risk, so it goes without saying that rubber gloves are pretty nifty, both in the operating room and in the doctor's office. Protective gloves prevent diseases like HIV, hepatitis, malaria, and influenza from being easily spread, especially in places like hospitals where there's a high chance there are people already infected.

Food Preparation: We come into contact with a lot of microbes and bacteria as we go about our day-to-day business. Thankfully for us (and our food), protective gloves in the food industry help drastically prevent the spread of bacteria like salmonella and E. coli from food-prep workers to the food itself.

Laboratory Settings: Deadly viruses, fatal diseases, caustic chemicals, and hazardous compounds all can be found in labs, and many of these are experimented on and studied by brave scientists and lab workers by hand. Nitrile gloves can be especially effective here, as they're more resistant to and less likely to absorb hazardous chemicals than latex.

this time did not know much about rubber or natural latex. Europeans were finally able to study the material and find new applications for it, such as in 1770 when British scientist Joseph Priestley and British engineer Edward Nairne discovered that rubber was perfect for erasing pencil marks. There was debate as to which of the two should really get credit for creating the eraser. Nairne was smart enough to manufacture and sell the product, though, and now holds the prestigious title of Inventor of the Eraser.

In the 1820s inventors started focusing on how to incorporate rubber into clothing in order to make them waterproof. A British industrialist discovered how to produce rubber threads; it wasn't long after that Charles Macintosh created the first raincoat. Like all good inventions, it happened by accident. While trying to find uses for the waste products generated in flammable gas factories, Macintosh saw that the byproducts

After collecting rubber latex from rubber trees, Mesoamericans would use it to make waterproof fabrics by coating fabric in the sap.

left behind after burning coal for fuel could dissolve natural rubber. He then took wool cloth, painted one side of it with the dissolved rubber, and put another layer of wool cloth on top. Voila! A waterproof jacket. They even named the garment a Mackintosh in honor of its inventor.

Of course, the raincoat wasn't perfect. Sometimes the oils in the wool caused the rubber to deteriorate, and sometimes tailors would puncture the fabric while seaming it. Both of these things made the coat not so waterproof anymore. Luckily, in 1839 Charles Goodyear stepped in to save the day, sort of. After multiple jail stints, years of poverty, and countless failed experiments, Goodyear accidentally threw a bunch of rubber on a stove and realized that the heated rubber had become waterproof.

Another inventor named Thomas Hancock made improvements to this rubber, just before

Left: Portrait of Charles Goodyear, inventor of rubber vulcanization. // Right: Waterproof rubber rain boots.

Goodyear's patent went through in England. The new manufacturing process for this tough and waterproof rubber would later be dubbed vulcanization, named after Vulcan, the Roman god of fire. A few years later, Stephen Perry used this process to invent and patent the world's first rubber band.

BRAZIL'S RUBBER

Let's leave Europe for a while and go back to South America, where rubber was old news by 1879. Thanks to the invention of a little thing called the automobile, however, the world suddenly had an even greater need for vast amounts of rubber. Remember all of those rubber trees in South America? Well, people living there quickly realized that they could make a lot of money by supplying this demand. Almost overnight, places like Manaus in Brazil transformed from tiny towns to busy centers of commerce. In fact, despite the fact that Manaus only had about 40,000 people living in

Left: A rubber-band ball.
// Right: An assortment of colored rubber bands—just one of the many ways we interact with rubber on a daily basis.

it, it had Brazil's first telephone system, 16 miles of streetcar tracks, and an electric grid more appropriate for a city of over 1 million.

Brazil didn't get to enjoy this rubber prosperity for long, though. In 1876 an English planter named Henry Wickham collected about 70,000 Hevea seeds and sent them back home to England. About 2,800 of these seeds were germinated and sent along to what is now Sri Lanka. The rubber plant didn't catch on right away, though, despite the success of the rubber market in South America. Planters in Asia were already successfully growing coffee and tea for profit, and had no interest in working with a plant that may or may not yield results. Finally, in 1895, Henry Ridley, the head of Singapore's botanical garden, convinced a couple of farmers to plant a few acres of Hevea trees.

Taking a Step Forward with Nike's Reuse-a-Shoe

NIKE'S ICONIC SLOGAN "Just Do It" takes on a whole new eco-meaning with the Reuse-a-Shoe program. Reuse-a-Shoe is a free recycling program for athletic shoes, which are so worn out they can no longer be donated. Annually the program recycles over 1.5 million pairs of shoes. Unfortunately, estimates show that over 300 million shoes are discarded annually in the U.S. alone.

When to Donate Shoes:
- The soles are not worn too thin.
- There are no significant rips or holes in the fabric.
- They're still in good shape, but you no longer like them.

When to Recycle Shoes:
- They're full of holes or are just too trashed to wear.

- The soles are worn out or the tread is gone.
- If the cushioning and/or support is completely worn out.

Nike takes the collected shoes and recycles them into Nike Grind, a proprietary material created from three parts of the shoes: rubber is extracted from the outer sole, foam from the inner sole, and fabric from the upper body. The grind is then used to produce athletic surfaces such as tennis courts and running tracks. Nike is also developing innovative uses for their grind to be used in footwear and apparel products.

Want to recycle your old athletic shoes? The program is completely free and accepts shoes of any brand. You can drop off up to ten pairs at most Nike or Converse retail locations. If you don't live near a store you can also mail your old shoes to Nike.

Left: During World War II, the British salvaged rubber from unwanted shoes and boots. // Below: Most modern shoes still have rubber soles.

Jump to 12 years later, and there were hundreds of thousands of acres of Hevea trees growing in Sri Lanka and Malaysia. Production increased rapidly, and at a fraction of the cost of collecting wild rubber in Brazil. In 1910, Brazilian rubber production had fallen 50 percent, and by 1940 their market share was down to 1.3 percent.

RUBBER PRODUCTION IN THE U.S.

The U.S. entered the rubber trade at the start of World War II. By this point, the vast majority of rubber was being produced in Southeast Asia. Unfortunately for the U.S., Japan occupied a lot of these rubber-producing areas; by 1942, the U.S. lost access to 90 percent of the world's natural rubber because of Japanese occupation. The Rubber Development Corporation looked for other sources of rubber, and funded expeditions into the Amazon to look for rubber specimens. Its goal was to establish rubber plantations closer to home, particularly in Latin America. The U.S. government also began to stockpile rubber, asking citizens to recycle their old tires, raincoats, gloves, hoses, and even rubber shoes for the good of the war effort.

SYNTHETIC RUBBER

Our focus thus far has been on natural rubber, but in the early 1900s both the U.S. and Germany were beginning to research means of producing synthetic rubber. In an attempt to make Germany self-sufficient, Hitler encouraged the German rubber industry, resulting in the creation of oil-resistant Buna N rubber in the 1930s. Standard Oil would buy out the German company IG Farben's right

Between 1976 and 2003, roughly 500 square miles of rainforest in China and other Southeast Asian countries were lost to make way for new rubber crops.

A Gas Mask requires 1.11 pounds of rubber

A Life Raft requires 17 to 100 pounds of rubber

A Scout Car requires 306 pounds of rubber

A Heavy Bomber requires 1,825 pounds of rubber

America needs your SCRAP RUBBER

World War II propaganda poster to promote the collection of rubber for the war effort in the U.S.

to the Buna N rubber, but after World War II America's access to natural rubber opened again and synthetic rubber became less of a priority. During the Korean War of the 1950s Americans were again cut off from the foreign market in natural rubber, forcing Americans to focus on the production of synthetic rubber.

Today, about 60 percent of rubber used around the world is synthetic. Around 80 percent of these synthetic rubbers are used by the automotive industry, particularly for car tires. The U.S. alone generates approximately 290 million scrap tires, 27 million of which end up in landfills. That doesn't include the scrap tires still unaccounted for in illegal tire dumps throughout the country.

RUBBER TIMELINE

1400 BCE The Olmec people of Meso-america use natural rubber from the rubber tree to create balls for a ceremonial ball game.

1745 Research by Charles-Marie de la Condamine suggests that tubing could be made from rubber due to its flexibility.

1823 Charles Macintosh creates the first raincoat by coating fabric with rubber.

1879 A massive rubber boom hits countries near the Amazon rainforest, home of the rubber-producing Hevea tree.

1525 CE Historian Padre d'Anghieria notices Mexican villagers playing with balls made from rubber, a material completely alien to Europeans at the time.

1770 Edward Nairne discovers rubber can erase pencil and invents the ubiquitous rubber pencil eraser.

1839 Charles Goodyear discovers that rubber and sulfur, when heated, produce a strong, durable rubber perfect for car tires. He calls the process "vulcanization."

1889 The first medical gloves used during surgery are sent to surgeon William Stewart Halsted by the Goodyear Company.

1845 Using Goodyear's vulcanization process, Stephen Perry invents and patents the rubber band.

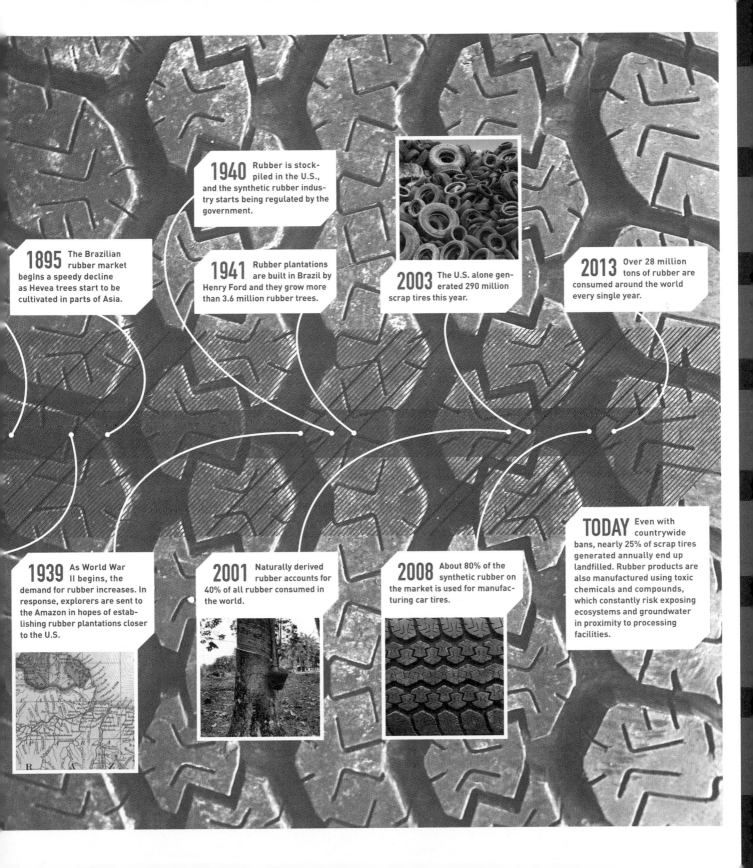

1895 The Brazilian rubber market begins a speedy decline as Hevea trees start to be cultivated in parts of Asia.

1940 Rubber is stockpiled in the U.S., and the synthetic rubber industry starts being regulated by the government.

1941 Rubber plantations are built in Brazil by Henry Ford and they grow more than 3.6 million rubber trees.

2003 The U.S. alone generated 290 million scrap tires this year.

2013 Over 28 million tons of rubber are consumed around the world every single year.

1939 As World War II begins, the demand for rubber increases. In response, explorers are sent to the Amazon in hopes of establishing rubber plantations closer to the U.S.

2001 Naturally derived rubber accounts for 40% of all rubber consumed in the world.

2008 About 80% of the synthetic rubber on the market is used for manufacturing car tires.

TODAY Even with countrywide bans, nearly 25% of scrap tires generated annually end up landfilled. Rubber products are also manufactured using toxic chemicals and compounds, which constantly risk exposing ecosystems and groundwater in proximity to processing facilities.

In 1990, there were only markets for 17 percent of scrap tire waste in the U.S., meaning that the vast majority of scrap tires ended up being landfilled. Fortunately, in 2003 demand rose to 80.4 percent, meaning that markets for scrap tires were now consuming 233 million of the 290 million scrap tires. So what are the different markets using these tire scraps for?

Here's a breakdown of what happens to scrap tires according to the Environmental Protection Agency:

- 44.7% (130 million): burned as fuel
- 19.4% (56 million): recycled or used in construction
- 7.8% (18 million): recycled into rubber mulch and products
- 4.3% (12 million): used for rubberized asphalt or are ground
- 3.1% (9 million): exported to other countries
- 2.0% (6.5 million): turned into stamped or cut products like shoe soles and floor mats.
- 1.7% (3 million): agricultural or other uses

That's a huge amount of waste that's been diverted from landfills in the U.S. Unfortunately, there are still tens of millions of tire scraps that get sent to landfills each year. Thirty-eight states ban whole scrap tires from being landfilled, as they can harm landfill covers with their uneven settlement and tendency to rise to the surface. Most scrap tires are chipped or ground down before getting sent to landfills or, more recently, monofills (a portion of a landfill dedicated to one type of material). Some are even utilized in the landfill, turned into capping and closures, as well as a material for daily cover.

Above: An assortment of rubber ducks. // Left: A tire yard in the 1940s. // Right: A modern tire recycling plant with tires waiting to be shredded.

Heap of old tires at a massive recycling plant in Thailand.

The "Rubber Capital of the World" is in Akron, Ohio, where Goodyear, Firestone, General Tire, and Goodrich were all founded. Today, Goodyear still has its headquarters in the city.

RUBBER TODAY

Tires are primarily made from synthetic rubber, but natural rubber is equally important to their production, along with many other rubber products.

Natural rubber comes from a variety of different trees and plants, and establishing large plantations to grow them is the most efficient method for harvesting the latex sap from the trees. In places like China, where unyielding growth in industry has caused massive spikes in raw material demand, huge tracts of natural forest are being replaced by these types of rubber plantations. Take the Xishuangbanna region in southern China, which was once full to the brim with tropical forestland. As the rubber boom got more intense, nearly a fifth of the region was replaced with rubber trees. Research from the Asia Development Bank found that every hectare of land cultivated for growing rubber loses about 20 tons of soil a year due to erosion.

An estimated 1.2 million acres of land in China, Cambodia, Thailand, Myanmar, Vietnam, and Laos have been transformed for rubber production, and by 2050 it could be two or even three times as much space. The increased presence of these plantations also saps water out of surrounding streams and rivers that are tapped into to irrigate dry tracts of land. The fertilizers, pesticides, and herbicides used by these plantations to protect their rubber trees can also pollute any water sources that happen to be nearby.

PRODUCING TIRES

Like almost any other product, making tires requires a lot of energy and resources, and can generate a significant amount of airborne pollutants. According to the Environmental Protection

Freitag

A TARP, a bicycle tire, and a car seat belt. Sounds like the first line to a bad joke or a very unusual shopping list, but for two Swiss brothers, it's the recipe for their business success. It was 1993 when Markus and Daniel Freitag, young graphic designers, longed for a durable and waterproof bicycle courier bag to tote drawings around. Inspired by the tarps used by highway tractor trailers to cover their cargo, the brothers combined used truck tarpaulins, old rubber bicycle inner tubes, and reclaimed car seat belts to produce the first of many FREITAG bags. Today, the business has been around for more than 20 years, sells 55 models of bags and accessories, and expanded to 10 FREITAG stores throughout Switzerland, Germany, Vienna, and Tokyo.

The Freitag brothers pride themselves on sustainable manufacturing. Each year, FREITAG gives a second chance to 440 tons of used truck tarps, 35,000 worn bicycle tires, and 288,000 recycled seat belts. The tarps are washed with collected rainwater before being hand-cut and sewn into shape. Seat belts provide the bags' straps, and the rubber bicycle tires provide extra strength as trimming for the finished bag. The bags can run a few hundred dollars a piece, so they are an investment—but if you have the means, you will be buying a waterproof, durable bag that you can depend on.

A FREITAG bike messenger bag made from used truck tarps.

Agency, the main environmental issues surrounding tire production are toxic air emissions, solid wastes (like tire scrap), wastewater (water tainted with chemicals and other compounds), and hazardous waste, all of which are produced right alongside your new car tires. The issues don't start and end with the production process, though. Tires are also made of a mix of rubber, petroleum, and "carbon black" filler, which is derived partially from burned fossil fuels. Even once they've gone through production, tires can still cause problems for the environment. Tires are meant to grip the road. After all, if they didn't, they wouldn't do us much good. But tires actually do too good of a job. They add so much friction that engines actually have to burn more fuel to overcome this. This extra fuel is responsible for about 86 percent of the greenhouse gas emissions that tires contribute.

LANDFILLS

In the U.S., almost a quarter of all tires produced end up in landfills, which is a problem for a number of reasons. Tires take a long time to decompose, and when they do finally break down, they release a lot of harmful components like oil and lead into the earth. Tires in landfills can also trap gases like

Left: Milk from a rubber tree harvested into a wooden bowl. Rubber is still extracted this way in many countries. // Right: A polluted river where fish are dying.

methane within their empty cavities, rather than allowing them to escape into the air. When these gases build up, the pressure can be so strong that it shoots the landfilled tire into the air! Because of the dangers associated with whole tires, a lot of states have banned them from being landfilled. In order for a tire to be sent to the dump, it usually has to be crushed or ground into smaller pieces first. A few states, however, still don't have any regulations on what can be landfilled.

TIRE FIRES

Though tires can be burned to make energy, this only works under very specific conditions. Most of the time, burning tires is a very bad idea. The smoke from tire fires can contain pollutants like polycyclic aromatic hydrocarbons (PAHs),

benzene, and butadiene, many of which have been linked to cancer (PAHs), neurological symptoms and blood disorders (benzene), and respiratory symptoms and cardiovascular disease (butadiene) in humans. Accidental tire fires in town stockpiles or illegal dumps also produce an oil runoff that, besides being highly flammable, threatens nearby water supplies with contaminants like lead and arsenic. For every million tires that are destroyed in these types of fires, 55,000 gallons of this runoff are produced. So just don't set tires on fire, you may be saying. Easier said than done. In 1999, a lightning strike in Westley, California, sparked a tire fire in a dump that contained millions of scrap tires. The air pollutants from the fire affected nearby farms and communities, and the runoff got into the drainage of an intermittent stream. It took 30 days to totally extinguish the fire, and the Environmental Protection Agency estimates that it cost $3.5 million to respond to the crisis.

RECYCLING TIRES

It's not all doom and gloom for the tire industry, however. Scrap tires are being reused in some pretty cool ways. Scrap tires can be shredded

CONTINUED ON PAGE 192 →

BICYCLE INNER TUBE WALLET

Getting tired of your old wallet? Make this upcycled bicycle tube wallet instead! It is thin, flexible, and will last a *wheelie* long time! For ages 12 and up.

WHAT YOU NEED

- Bicycle inner tube
- Scissors
- Rotary cutter
- Cutting mat
- Ruler
- ⅛-inch hole punch
- Binder clips

Cut your inner tube near the valve stem to maximize the usable length of the tube.

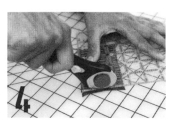

Cut two 4-inch and two 9-inch lengths of inner tube. Then cut open the four pieces vertically. Clean the talcum powder with soap and water.

Out of the two larger pieces, cut two identical 8 x 3¾-inch rectangles.

Cut the two smaller pieces into two identical 3¾ x 2½-inch rectangles; these will form your card pockets.

5 Cut a curve on one corner of each of the pocket pieces.

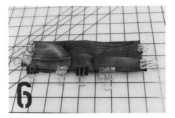

6 Lay all of your pieces as shown, and use the binder clips to hold them in place.

7 Using the remaining piece of your inner tube, cut an 18-inch-long section, slice it open, and clean.

8 Use a ruler to cut two 1/8-inch strips out of the 18-inch section. These will form the "thread" to lace the wallet.

9 Punch holes every ¼ inch around the side and bottom of your wallet. Then, lace the long strip through, starting on one of the upper corners. Make sure to securely tie a knot through the first two holes.

10 When you reach the halfway point of the wallet, make a double knot and loop back through.

11 From the opposite corner, repeat steps 9 and 10. Make sure your knots are securely in place, and then snip any excess.

FINISHED

MAKING CAR TIRES...
FROM DANDELIONS???

Car tires are one of the most ubiquitous and visceral forms of waste. Everyone can picture the huge piles of used tires at junkyards or landfills. The numbers are as eye-opening as the unsightly piles themselves. In the U.S. and Europe, over 500 million tires are discarded every year, totaling well over 10 billion pounds of rubber waste.

Suddenly, an environmentally and socially responsible solution is sprouting up. The lowly dandelion, a much-maligned flower traditionally known as a bothersome weed, is being explored as an economically viable source of rubber.

This wouldn't be the first time dandelions were called on to replace the rubber tree. During World War II, trade with Asia collapsed, forcing the Soviet Union, Europe, and the U.S. to cultivate the Kazakh dandelion *(Taraxacum kok-saghyz)* to help develop an emergency supply of rubber. After the war, trading was normalized and the dandelion was relegated back to inconsequential status.

Fast forward to 2007, when consumers began to demand more domestically sourced, socially responsible products. A team of researchers at Ohio State University began to re-explore what steps would be necessary to make dandelions a viable source of rubber. They partnered with major tire manufacturers such as Bridgestone to create the Program of Excellence in Natural Rubber Alternatives. Similar partnerships between tire manufacturers and researchers are taking place across Europe.

While the developers are tight-lipped on the exact process, various known ways include grinding the flower's taproot into a pulp, which can be processed into natural rubber. The team at Ohio State University is on track to develop a viable business model by 2020, which will allow dandelions to produce the same amount of natural rubber per acre as the best Asian rubber tree plantations (roughly 3,300 pounds).

Who knows, by the time you buy your next car, it might roll off the lot on a set of flower-root tires!

The New American finds his challenge and his love in the traffic-choked streets, skies nested in smog, choking with the acids of industry, the screech of rubber and houses leashed in against one another while the townlets wither a time and die.

—JOHN STEINBECK

and used along with concrete aggregate, cement, and water to make absorptive sound barriers for highways. A number of different brands of resilient playground rubber surfacing material are also using recycled tires to make products. In 2001, about 80 million pounds of scrap tire rubber was used for rubber turf. Scrap tires are also being used for flooring, soil additives, and landfill construction materials.

To recycle your used tires, call your local tire retailer or recycling facility and find out if old tires are accepted. Your local municipality may even hold "tire amnesty days" where you can bring in your used tires free of charge!

LOOKING FORWARD

TerraCycle got involved with the rubber waste stream through an unlikely product: shoes. The rubber soles of a shoe need to be strong enough to last through heavy wear and tear, so many are made with synthetic rubber, or the same rubber used to produce car tires. This makes the material very durable, and equally resilient to weathering and degradation. To get involved we first launched both retail-based and mail-in collection programs for this waste stream.

Once collected, the shoes are primarily reused, cleaned, and resold to countries where people can't afford a new pair of shoes; the collected flip-flops are recycled by shredding and melting them into a plastic compound that has gone into making a number of children's playgrounds as well as a host of other products.

There are so many applications for rubber that even the chewing gum we avoid while walking on the sidewalk is made from it. The gum base of chewing gum is a naturally sourced or synthetically produced rubber (which is why it doesn't dissolve as you chew it). Because it's essentially just another durable rubber product, it won't naturally decompose in the environment, costing cities tens of millions of dollars a year to clean off sidewalks and dispose of properly. To help combat this issue

Your favorite chewing gum owes its invention to the latex ("chicle") in Mexican sapodilla trees.

Chewing gum stuck to a wall at Pike Place Market in Seattle has become a tourist attraction.

TerraCycle employees made a statue from tires and a car. It's displayed in the courtyard of the head-quarters in New Jersey. // Page 195: A rubber plantation.

we developed a method to recycle used chewing gum, in which it is reprocessed into a polymer that we can make almost any plastic product from.

As with just about any object, the best solution is to think about whether you really need to buy the product. If you do end up buying something new, try to buy something that is durable and will last you a long time, reducing the need to replace it multiple times.

WHAT YOU CAN DO

Car tires are a good place to start, and many municipalities have locations where used tires can be disposed of. Some are completely free, some require payment, and some still will even pay you for tires that are good enough to be retreaded.

There is a large enough market for scrap tires that even some tire manufacturers accept them from consumers. Liberty Tire Recycling (libertytire.com) is one example, and you can check out the list of recycling locations on their website to see if there is one near you.

Shoes, another source of rubber waste, can be donated. Old pairs that are still in relatively good shape maintain their economic value, and can be diverted from landfills. Soles 4 Souls (soles4souls.org) accepts shoes and clothing of all types, and you can ship to them for free. The Salvation Army, Goodwill Industries International, and thrift stores are also good alternatives if the shoes are still in wearable condition.

Rubber has a lot in common with plastic, especially in that it will not degrade once it's in the environment. That's why even a single shoe tossed into roadside brush is a potential hazard, as the sole will remain intact for hundreds of years. Rubber bands deteriorate when they are exposed to oxygen, but again they don't disappear or biodegrade like organic waste generally will. Even the chewing gum that's spit onto our sidewalks would remain there if municipalities didn't pay millions of dollars every year to have it all removed. We leave our mark everywhere we step, and it's time to start realizing it.

LIFECYCLE OF A TIRE

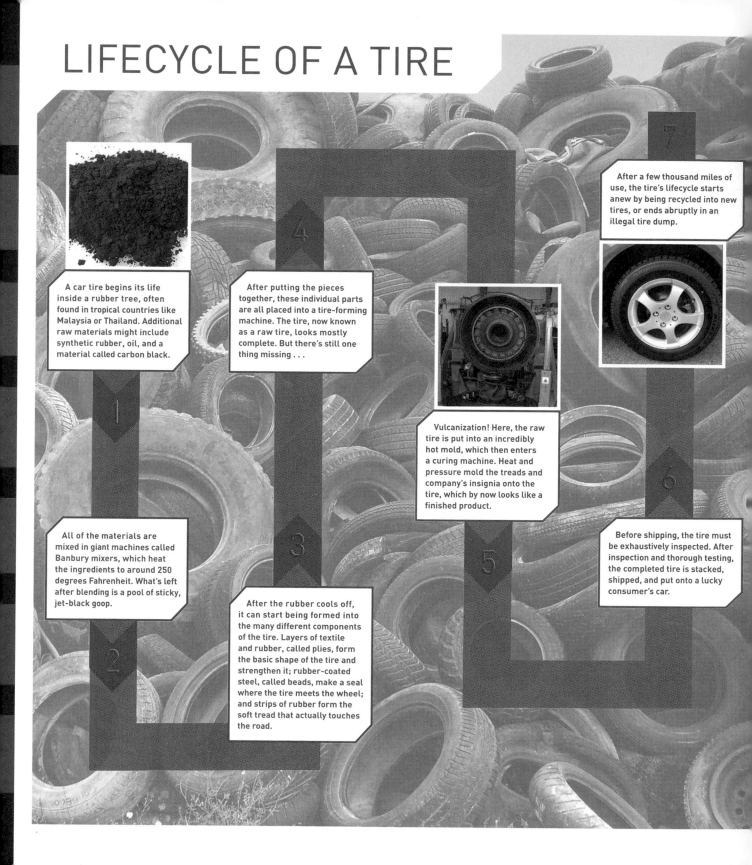

1 — A car tire begins its life inside a rubber tree, often found in tropical countries like Malaysia or Thailand. Additional raw materials might include synthetic rubber, oil, and a material called carbon black.

2 — All of the materials are mixed in giant machines called Banbury mixers, which heat the ingredients to around 250 degrees Fahrenheit. What's left after blending is a pool of sticky, jet-black goop.

3 — After the rubber cools off, it can start being formed into the many different components of the tire. Layers of textile and rubber, called plies, form the basic shape of the tire and strengthen it; rubber-coated steel, called beads, make a seal where the tire meets the wheel; and strips of rubber form the soft tread that actually touches the road.

4 — After putting the pieces together, these individual parts are all placed into a tire-forming machine. The tire, now known as a raw tire, looks mostly complete. But there's still one thing missing . . .

5 — Vulcanization! Here, the raw tire is put into an incredibly hot mold, which then enters a curing machine. Heat and pressure mold the treads and company's insignia onto the tire, which by now looks like a finished product.

6 — Before shipping, the tire must be exhaustively inspected. After inspection and thorough testing, the completed tire is stacked, shipped, and put onto a lucky consumer's car.

7 — After a few thousand miles of use, the tire's lifecycle starts anew by being recycled into new tires, or ends abruptly in an illegal tire dump.

> At first I thought I was fighting to save rubber trees, then I thought I was fighting to save the Amazon rainforest. Now I realize I am fighting for humanity.
>
> —CHICO MENDES, ENVIRONMENTALIST

When tapped, a rubber tree will drip latex for about 4 hours before stopping, and each tree will produce for up to 35 years. The average rubber tapper can collect latex from 450 trees per day.

If we want to lower incidences of autism, learning disorders, diabetes, cancer, coronary heart disease, allergies, osteoporosis, migraines, dementia, and hyperactivity, we should be eating organic!

CHAPTER 8

ORGANICS

Consumers in the U.S. throw away about 36 million tons of food every year. About 40 percent of the food produced in the U.S., valued at around $165 billion, ends up being thrown away without even being consumed. Considering the average American eats one ton of food per year (about five and a half pounds, or 2,700 calories, a day), that means the U.S. could feed 36 million people massive portions of food for a year with all of the food that is thrown out. Every time you dump your uneaten scraps into the trash after dinner, or toss an expired loaf of bread into the garbage bin, you are contributing to the

largest category of waste sent to landfills every year. Making matters worse, most people don't think throwing half-eaten food away is a major issue. Consumers might not be to blame; there is no easy way to take your meatloaf scraps to a food bank or needy family. Part of the way to deal with the issue is to plan better and purchase and cook only what you need. Just those simple steps will help reduce food waste in the household.

It wasn't always like this. There once was a time when food was difficult to come by. Humans used to struggle from season to season to find reliable (and varied) sources of food, all while dodging predators and competing with other groups of humans. Any scrap of food that was collected was coveted for being the life-giving nutrient it was, and everything that could be used was consumed. It was as natural and sustainable a society as humans have ever been.

Things look different thousands of years later in the twenty-first century, where processed and mass-produced food, some that originated halfway across the world, can be bought at any corner store down the block. Careful collection and preservation is no longer needed, and cheap disposability has become more of a necessity to people, rather than just a consumer preference. The result: a lot of organic waste.

THE DAWN OF DINING

The shift toward disposability and wastefulness didn't happen overnight. It wasn't until the Neolithic Revolution over 10,000 years ago that people

One beef patty can contain meat from 55 to more than a thousand cattle from five different countries.

Previous spread: Compost bin; organic food stand (*inset*). // Above: A line drawing from 1873 showing walled-in farmland. // Left: TerraCycle's first product was an organic fertilizer made from worm poop.

Bullocks with yoke to pull the plow, a traditional style of agriculture still practiced in some parts of Italy.

Organics have been found to be 25% more nutritious than products made from industrial agriculture. At least in terms of vitamins and minerals!

even began to understand and utilize agriculture, shifting away from the hunter-gatherer lifestyle to live in more permanent farming communities. On the not-so-exciting menu: barley, lentils, flax, wheat, chickpeas, and other grains and legumes. Anything that could be domesticized and cultivated in bulk would ensure that a community could be fed for months or years, weather permitting. It was the first time in human history that food was being reliably (for the most part) produced in large quantities for an entire community or population. Goodbye nomadic lifestyle; hello agricultural revolution!

From the Neolithic Revolution onward, people began to expand and develop agriculture to manage growing populations and the need for more varied food sources. By 7000 BCE, people had already begun raising livestock like pigs and sheep, and an early version of the plow for sowing fields was starting to be commonly used. Basic forms of irrigation were developed in Mesopotamia in 5500

BCE, finally allowing crops to be cultivated in areas where fertility of the land was questionable. A bit more than a thousand years after that, specialized plows were being made for livestock like cattle, ramping up food production once again.

Farmers somehow realized that their livestock's poop could be used to fertilize the very seeds they were helping to sow. This animal waste became an integral part of the farming process; it found a use for the organic waste produced by livestock like cattle, while subsequently aiding in the growth of new crops. Like we did at TerraCycle with worm poop, ancient farmers did with livestock manure, the only difference being that they needed it to fertilize crops necessary to sustain their entire population.

Ancient civilizations—Romans, Egyptians, Greeks—were dependent on agriculture for trade and for their own populations, and developments in farming technology facilitated the growth of the civilizations. Crop rotation was one of those

Left: Ancient Egyptian wall painting of grain being harvested by workers and cattle. // Below: Medieval painting of a fifteenth-century French banquet.

developments, and variants of it were extensively used in ancient Greece and Rome. Crop rotation is a simple system: farmers rotate which fields they keep fallow (unplanted) and which they grow crops in. Once crops are harvested, they rotate fields and grow in the previously fallow field. This prevents the soil from being depleted of all its nutrients, while subsequently disrupting any pests who may reside in the soil. Little is known about ancient crop rotation practices, but we do know that a two-field system of crop rotation spread to parts of western Europe by 800 CE.

FOOD PRESERVATION

It was discovered early on that salting food was an excellent form of preservation, essentially dehydrating food to the point that mold and bacteria are unable to grow. Salt really became an indispensable and highly valued commodity, partially because of its food preservation benefits, along with its many other applications.

Some early barbarian cultures in Europe had an interesting form of preserving food: glorifying the high-volume consumption of it. Many of these groups—the Celts, for example—relied on foraging and hunting to sustain their population. Warriors would establish their social status by eating large

quantities of food, which was also the case because food was scarce in general. The result was an extremely limited amount of food waste, and bands of warriors with fat bellies.

Food was preserved in China at least from the second century on. Fish was a huge staple of the region's diet, so it was important to ensure that stores of fish could last for an extended period of time. Their solution was to put slabs of fish onto beds of rice, salt, and a large rock. The fish would essentially ferment, allowing it to last for months, to even years. The fish would be preserved, but the rice was usually discarded.

Preservation was not widely practiced in many parts of Europe during the first few

FIVE WAYS TO WASTE LESS FOOD

We waste a lot of food. With supermarkets packed full of cheap brands and packaged goods, it's no wonder we overconsume and overdispose. These are a few easy ways that you can lower your household's food waste without any drastic changes to your lifestyle.

1 Buy Smart: It's pretty simple: if you buy less unnecessary food, you and your family will waste less. You can also stock up on baking and cooking supplies so that you aren't so reliant on pre-made packaged goods to feed your family.

2 Know What Dates Mean: Not every date printed onto a food package is an expiration date. A "sell by" date, for example, simply indicates when a product isn't considered at peak quality anymore, and should be taken off the shelf. "Best if used by" dates are again for quality assurance, when a product should be consumed for maximum quality and freshness. More often than not, dates like these are quality suggestions, not when a product truly expires. Use common sense and, depending on the product and how perishable it is, don't always blindly adhere to the printed dates.

3 Buy Local Produce: Whether at a farmers' market, CSA, or local farm stand, produce that you buy fresh and locally can cut down on your food waste. Make smaller weekly purchases so that you have a constant supply of fresh produce that doesn't get wasted. Local produce often costs less than supermarket produce, so you can save money, too.

4 Preserve: It goes without saying that you should capitalize on leftovers whenever possible, but preserving food for the long-term isn't difficult either. The freezer is your friend, as are airtight containers. Pickling and canning food can make food last incredible lengths of time, but only attempt either if you know what you are doing and have reliable guidelines to follow.

5 Compost: When all else fails, start composting old food. It's a great way to utilize food scraps instead of wasting them, and your garden gets to see the benefits. Just remember, anything oily or laced with harsh chemicals should never end up in your compost bin.

centuries, as famine, war, and other widespread conflicts limited the availability of labor and degraded infrastructure. As food supplies dwindled, people relied on whatever food they could get their hands on and eat immediately; storing food for extended periods of time was not practical. The solution for food shortages in Europe was often to require farmers to produce wheat to increase the supply of bread, while wealthy aristocrats were still able to eat meat several times a week. An abundance of a variety of food was considered such a status symbol that eating leftovers for dinner was frowned upon as a sign of impoverishment. In fact, some aristocratic and royal circles purposefully overproduced meals to put on display, making banquets and lavish dinners look even more grandiose and exquisite. Practices like these were so prevalent and wasteful that in 1356, a requirement to regulate and limit the number of meals during banquets and other extravagant events was imposed in Florence, Italy.

Leftover food from the circles of aristocracy and royalty was often given to impoverished communities, limiting the amount of food that ended up getting thrown away, even if it was possibly moldy or spoiled. Food was so important that as much as 80 percent of a family's funds could be used as the food budget during the Middle Ages. Leftovers were saved and preserved in many places by mixing them with vinegar for later consumption. Austrian restaurants in the eighteenth century found a unique way to utilize leftover food from the Imperial Court, by integrating it into their menus and serving it to lower-income populations. These Viennese restaurants were so popular and successful that they could donate proceeds to orphans, beggars, and hospitals, all while feeding the workers and laborers who themselves worked at the restaurant.

A FOOD REVOLUTION

Preserving food was important when food was scarce and not reliably available, but that changed when food became easier to produce around the middle of the seventeenth century. Also known as

Wasted-food costs for the U.S. are about $165 billion per year, $40 billion of which comes from household waste. Each year $750 million is spent to get rid of the food that we throw in the trash.

the second Agricultural Revolution, farming technology and more efficient agricultural practices started to take over across the world. It's important to note here, however, that different agricultural revolutions spread at different rates, depending on geographic region. Still for the most part, more efficient agricultural practices spread quickly. Food could be produced so efficiently that, for the first time, surpluses were accumulating. From the 1701 invention of the seed drill, which automatically planted and covered seeds, to Charles Townshend's

Left: Portrait of Charles Townshend. // Right: Drawing of a seed drill, first published in 1910 in the book *Meyers Konversations-Lexikon*, volume 7, Leipzig, Germany.

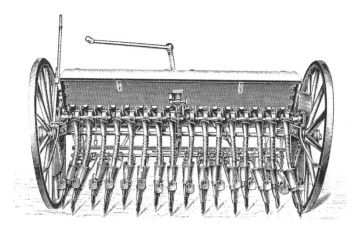

Organic foods' cost on average about 20% higher than their conventional foods.

A traditional motorized tractor, now rusted and no longer working.

four-field crop-rotation system, farmers could aggressively grow their productivity.

We've now arrived at the nineteenth century, where an onslaught of mass-production technology began to take root. Cyrus McCormick invented the first mechanical reaper in 1831, decreasing the amount of labor needed to harvest crops, while subsequently increasing the acreage one farmer could cover in a day. Only a few years later, John Deere invented a plow made from steel, further increasing production rates, also leading to his eponymous brand of agricultural machines and products. With the development of superphosphate, an important component of man-made fertilizers, farmers no longer had to depend on natural organic waste from their livestock, and could instead take a trip to the store.

A seemingly innocuous, yet revolutionary development in 1881 marks one of the biggest advances in the food industry to date: hybrid corn. Just think about it—without the massive availability of corn that we have today, a majority of the food products sitting on store shelves wouldn't exist. High-fructose corn syrup, for example, is cheap compared with sugar, in part because corn is widely available and economical to grow. By growing hybrid variants of crops that are prone to high yields and quick growing cycles, productivity and food manufacturing expanded.

The second Industrial Revolution spurred growth in just about every major global industry, including agriculture. The influx of new technology and mechanized parts led to the invention of efficient machines like the combine crop harvester, which lowered the time needed to harvest wheat and similar crops by 80 percent. Only a few years

ORGANICS TIMELINE

800 Two-field crop rotation is first used in western Europe, preserving fields and increasing crop yields.

10,000 BCE The Neolithic Revolution begins, as humans transition from nomadic lives to sedentary farming communities, domesticating crops like barley, lentils, and flax.

6000 The power of poop! Ancient farmers begin using manure as a common fertilizer for their crops.

1650 The second Agricultural Revolution begins. Better technology practically doubled productivity, leading to agricultural surpluses for the first time in many regions of the world.

1750 Charles Townshend introduces the four-field crop-rotation system, improving soil quality, limiting damage from crop pests, and increasing overall yields.

7000 The plow appears for the first time, transforming agriculture and significantly increasing production.

5500 Irrigation is practiced in Mesopotamia, allowing farmlands to develop in areas that were previously not fertile enough.

1 CE The Kallanai Dam, one of the oldest dams still in use, is built in India. Dams were revolutionary, allowing water to be stored for agricultural use for great lengths of time.

1701 The seed drill is introduced by English agriculturalist Jethro Tull as a new, quick method of planting that required far less manual labor.

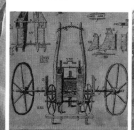

1809 "Canning" is invented in France by chef and distiller Nicolas Appert as a way to preserve food longer, cutting down waste from food that spoiled quickly.

1843 English agriculturist Sir John Lawes develops superphosphate, a precursor to the commercial fertilizer industry.

1892 The first gasoline-powered tractor is built by American inventor John Froelich.

2002 TerraCycle purchases a machine capable of using organic waste to feed worms, leading to TerraCycle's first line of organic worm-poop plant-food fertilizers.

2010 Composting, the ultimate solution to organic waste, is practiced by only 8% of Americans.

1881 The first generation of high-yielding hybrid corn is developed.

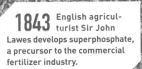

1944 The Green Revolution begins. This time of research, development, and innovations will drastically increase agricultural production in the coming decades.

2009 San Francisco is the first city in the U.S. to make composting mandatory for all citizens.

TODAY Each year, about 40% of food produced in the U.S. goes to waste. That's equivalent to $165 billion wasted. Globally, 1.4 billion tons of food is wasted every year, most in the beginning of the food production process itself.

1974 Nearly 28% of food produced in the U.S. is thrown away, sent away to rot in landfills.

1890 The combine harvester is used for the first time, reducing the amount of time needed to harvest one hectare, or about 2.5 acres, of wheat by 80%.

later, the first gasoline-powered farm tractor was invented. Human labor was slowly being replaced by machines, and automated technology was vastly improving the viability of mass production.

Rosemary oils can be used as a meat preservative that works better than chemical additives.

GREEN REVOLUTION

By the early twentieth century and the onset of World War II, the world was in dire straits. Violence and conflict, as well as a general degradation of infrastructure, led to food shortages and starving populations in many parts of the world. Even once the war was over, many parts of the war-scorched world struggled to maintain proper levels of food. The response to this global struggle was the postwar "Green Revolution," a global effort to research new varieties of crops that, through genetic engineering, could be higher yielding. Developments in agricultural technology led to better pesticides, improved crops, and even fertilizers. The benefits of these new technologies and products would span the globe, helping struggling populations everywhere increase production and lower the cost of food.

Today we grow enough grain to feed every human being about 3,500 calories every day, while at the same time global hunger and starvation have actually increased since the Green Revolution started seventy years ago. Approximately 35 million tons of food end up landfill-bound in the U.S. every year.

Even organic waste has value, you just have to know how to unlock it. Take something like TerraCycle's worm poop plant food. We took food scraps, fed it to worms, and collected the worms' poop to use it as an effective fertilizer. This prevents the organic waste from becoming landfill, where it would release methane into the atmosphere. Instead, we give it new life with new economic value as a useful product.

So next time you contemplate throwing some leftovers in the trash, just realize that you are wasting a potentially useful material, and contributing to one of the biggest waste streams on the planet.

Plant parsley to save your garden! Parsley attracts predatory insects that will eat the pests that are going after your other plants. You can also sprinkle your plants with parsley leaves.

Right: Men in a bread line during the Great Depression in the U.S. // Above: A bunch of rosemary ready to be picked.

FIVE THINGS YOU DIDN'T KNOW COULD BE MADE FROM ORGANIC MATERIALS

1 **Tennis Racket String** (Cow Intestines): Many tennis players insist that racket strings made out of animal intestines make for the best, highest-quality rackets you can buy. Known as "natural gut," it can take the intestines of as many as four different cows to string just one tennis racket.

2 **Fire Extinguishing Foam** (Livestock Hooves): The hooves of animals like cattle are packed with keratin, the protein that gives your fingernails and hair structure and flexibility. When used in a foam-making fire extinguisher, the keratin helps keep the foam bonded together in a sheet, which essentially smothers the life out of any fire that gets in its way.

3 **Face Cream** (Sheep Placenta): You didn't misread anything, there is a decent-size market for face cream made out of the placenta of a sheep. The idea is that the stem cells within the placenta can help repair old cells and eliminate wrinkles. There are plenty of skeptics, and for good reason: It costs over $350 for less than an ounce of the stuff.

4 **Food Coloring** (Crushed Insects): If you've ever eaten something with red food coloring or dye, there's a good chance it was made by crushing insects, specifically *Dactylopius coccus*. Look under the ingredients—if you see carmine, cochineal, or carminic acid, you've been eating crushed bugs. But don't worry, they are completely harmless.

5 **Hair Gel** (Shrimp Shells): A shrimp's hard outer shell is full of a type of organic polymer called chitin, what a crab or lobster's shell is also made out of. Adding this chitin to products like hair gels and styling creams can give your hair more volume, make it shinier, and prevent split ends from forming.

A commercial wheat harvesting combine being used to deliver harvested wheat.

ORGANICS TODAY

Did your parents ever demand you eat everything on your plate, because hungry kids in less privileged parts of the world were starving? Even if they were just trying to get you to eat your broccoli, they really did have a point: there are close to 1 billion starving and hungry people on the planet, the vast majority of them in developing countries in regions like Latin America, Asia, Africa, and the Pacific. Even in the developed world where food is supposed to be plentiful there are 16 million people in need of food.

About 1.4 billion tons of food waste is generated every year, which is around one-third of all food produced annually. The same amount (one-third) is thrown away in the U.S. every year, valued somewhere around $48 billion. That's more than two and a half times as much as NASA's entire budget for 2015, all of which could have gone to facilitate ending the starvation of millions of people.

Apart from the humanitarian crisis catalyzed by high levels of wasted food, a toll is also taken on the environment due to the sheer volume of food and other organic waste materials left in landfills. You might think that because organic waste is easily biodegradable, there are extremely limited risks to the environment. This is one of the biggest misconceptions that many consumers have about food waste, as they think scraps and leftovers tossed in the garbage bin will simply decompose naturally like most organic waste does in nature. But when we're talking about landfills, the story can be entirely different.

WHAT HAPPENS IN LANDFILLS

Normally, organic waste that is left to decompose out in the open will decompose and release carbon dioxide, as oxygen is present. If your rotting Thanksgiving leftovers are deep within landfills, the lack of oxygen will cause the food to decompose and release methane into the atmosphere. Methane is 21 times more potent than carbon dioxide when it comes to global warming. It can be a great source of energy if captured and prevented from entering the atmosphere, but not so much floating freely in the air. There is so much organic waste in U.S. landfills that they account for 20 percent of all emissions of methane in the country. Home and municipal-level composting could alleviate much of this stress on the environment, but as it stands only about 35 percent of the food waste generated (in the U.S., at least) is composted.

The methane organic waste produces is dangerous in more ways than one; did you know that landfill methane, when not properly managed, can seep into nearby buildings, sometimes even to such high levels that it can pose an explosion risk? Methane (which can be highly flammable in these contexts as well) and other landfill gases can even move through the soil into nearby basements and utility stations. Think of it as the collective ghost of all the leftover food that was good enough only for the trash bin.

How and why has the level of organic waste gotten to be like this? For starters, the international market for processed food products stands at approximately $3.2 trillion, which is about 75 percent of annual global food sales. Food products and fast-food companies dominate the marketing arena as well, influencing millions of people as they watch TV, listen to the radio, or look through

A homeless man begs for food and money. Hunger and malnutrition are the biggest issues facing the homeless.

Fast-food corporations use 50 different chemicals to make their strawberry flavoring.

FOUR WAYS TO MAKE COMPOSTING FUN FOR KIDS

Composting is amazing for the environment, but can often feel like a tedious chore to children. Engaging kids and getting them excited to compost is easier than it sounds, and here are a few ways to start.

1 Educate Them: Teaching kids what composting is and how to do it can pique their interest and demonstrate how easy it really is to do. To start, you can paint or craft a poster with them that shows what food items they can throw into the organics bin. Tell them that the food they throw away will get moldy and rot anyway, and that composting is a way to make leftover food helpful even when it is long past being edible.

2 Dig Through the Compost: Getting down and dirty to show your kids what's in the compost pile can be a fun (maybe a little gross) experience. Show them the hundreds of small creatures, worms, and organisms that help decompose organic waste in the compost pile to really get them intrigued. This will let them see firsthand what their leftover food scraps are turning into.

3 Let Them Work the Pile: Whether they add food to the pile or help you turn it, getting them directly involved shows them how easy composting really is. You can assign a child a certain duty to be responsible for, such as emptying the organic waste bin into the pile, so they feel a sense of ownership over the composting process. Doing everything together can also present composting as more of a fun activity, not a chore.

4 Use the Compost: Once you have some finished compost, work with the kids in the garden and start using it! If they've been helping from the beginning, they will get to see the end product they helped to create in action.

magazines. In 2009, for example, fast-food companies spent $4.2 billion just on advertising. A 2006 study from the *Journal of Public Health Policy* estimates that nearly $10 billion is spent every year in the food industry to advertise to kids, usually for unhealthy packaged and processed foods like candy, salty snacks, and sugary cereal. Many of these products are so profitable because they are made with unhealthy, but cheap, crops that are subsidized by the government. Corn, wheat, and similar crops dominate the product market because they are cheap and can be processed at little cost, but in high volume. The result: grocery store shelves lined with unhealthy, dirt-cheap food products that facilitate our desire for convenience and carefree disposal.

The meat industry in the U.S. generates 61 million tons of animal waste every year, polluting rivers and groundwater. In fact, the Environmental Protection Agency reports that this type of animal waste pollutes nearly 35,000 miles of river in the U.S. Manure contains microorganisms that are dangerous to humans and other wildlife. In 1991, about 1 billion fish were killed by these types of microorganisms in North Carolina alone.

It's a shame, because animal waste can be an extremely useful material in the right applications (remember the worm-poop fertilizer mentioned previously). When the food industry fails to manage the waste caused by their products and by the actual production process itself, a potentially useful product is needlessly lost, and the environment is forced to pay the price.

LOOKING FORWARD

TerraCycle can trace its history back to the days when we were turning Princeton University's cafeteria food waste into worm poop (or vermicompost) via red worms. The resulting worm poop

Our grandparents used to make a point of not throwing away leftover food. Consumerism has made us accustomed to wasting food daily and we are unable to see its real value.

— POPE FRANCIS

A compost pile with organic waste.

EGGSHELL PLANTER

The next time you are making scrambled eggs or quiche, save the shells and the cardboard carton to make a beautiful mini succulent planter! They make perfect little gifts or party favors. For ages 12 and up.

WHAT YOU NEED

- 1 dozen eggs
- Cardboard egg carton
- 12 small succulents or other plants
- Soil
- Spanish moss (optional)
- Spoon
- Skewer or fork

Using the skewer or fork tip, gently poke a small hole in the top of an egg. Carefully increase the size of the hole to about ½ inch, then drain the egg into a bowl for later use. Repeat with the rest of the eggs.

Gently increase the hole size on each egg until the opening is large enough for planting.

TIP: THIS MAKES A GREAT SEED STARTER KIT! WHEN THE SEEDLINGS GROW, PLANT THEM DIRECTLY INTO THE GROUND, CARDBOARD AND ALL!

Spoon a small amount of soil into the egg, and then gently place a plant inside. Add a little more soil to fill in around it. Tamp down gently.

Add a small amount of Spanish moss to fill in empty areas, then place your eggs into the carton. Enjoy your new planter as is, or place the eggs directly into the soil outside.

A meat display at a typical supermarket.

is an incredibly effective fertilizer, and all it took to make was some soon-to-be-trashed slop from a cafeteria garbage bin. It was a sustainable, environmentally friendly manufacturing process, and we were even generating revenue from it. Eliminating the idea of waste became a central tenet of TerraCycle's business model after that. We could take waste and inject economic value back into it. It was no longer "garbage," but a seemingly endless pool of untapped resources.

Beyond TerraCycle, the best way to deal with organic waste is to compost it at home (that is if you don't have a green bin to put it into where you live). To make this easy there are a wide range of composters easily available, from small vermicomposting units for your small apartment to large outdoor units for your larger home.

And, as always, remember to buy smart to avoid having any food waste.

WHAT YOU CAN DO
Composting is one of the best, simplest ways to utilize organic waste. So instead of having a single trash bin, have one for solid waste and a separate one for organic waste. As long as it isn't meat or fish (including bones and skin), a dairy product, and isn't oily or greasy, you should be able to

compost it. Once you've collected a good amount of organic scrap, you need to get yourself a composter, or make a simple compost pile. Additives like humus, sawdust, or peat moss will also help turn the mixture into compost. Then, it's just a matter of buying a composter or building yourself a compost pile.

The Gardener's Supply Company (gardeners.com) is a great resource to use to find the best composter for you and your family. Some are so small and efficient that they can be used to make small quantities of compost right in your kitchen, while others are big enough for only the most serious of composters. You really have no excuse not to compost anymore, as there are countless sizes, variations, and styles available. We turned old wine barrels from Napa Valley into our own TerraCycle

A selection of fruits and vegetables at a supermarket.

brand of rotary composter, sometimes called a batch composter.

Composting might not be for everyone, and if that's the case there are still ways to reduce organic waste accumulation in socially responsible ways. In the U.S., foodpantries.org allows you to search your state for food pantries around you, so you can give away your good, but unwanted, food before it goes bad. Feeding America (feedingamerica.org) is a similar nonprofit, hoping to raise money and food for starving Americans. Again, prevent that unwanted food from feeding a landfill, and feed someone who actually needs it instead.

The Hunger Project is one of the best global nonprofits hoping to end world hunger. Sustainability is even one of the organization's ten primary principles: "Solutions to ending hunger must be sustainable locally, socially, economically, and environmentally." That's right from their webpage (thp.org), so go check it out to see how you can become a part of their incredible mission.

For most of us in developed regions of the globe, a plate of half-eaten dinner dregs being spooned into the garbage bin often doesn't feel as alarming as it should. We do it unconsciously without thinking most of the time, as there aren't many clear alternatives staring us directly in the face. Thankfully, municipalities in all parts of the world are starting to pick up the slack, creating a recycling or composting infrastructure that allows organic waste to be collected directly from the homes that generate it. The town where I spent my college days, Princeton, New Jersey, is one of many municipalities in the U.S. that is beginning to offer curbside organic pickup as citizens increasingly demand them. San Francisco even requires its citizens to separate compostable waste from solid waste. Alongside the blue recycling bin and black garbage bin, more and more cities are starting to introduce the green bin. It's a refreshing push toward sustainability that people are starting to demand from their state representatives, and you can do the same.

LIFECYCLE OF A BANANA

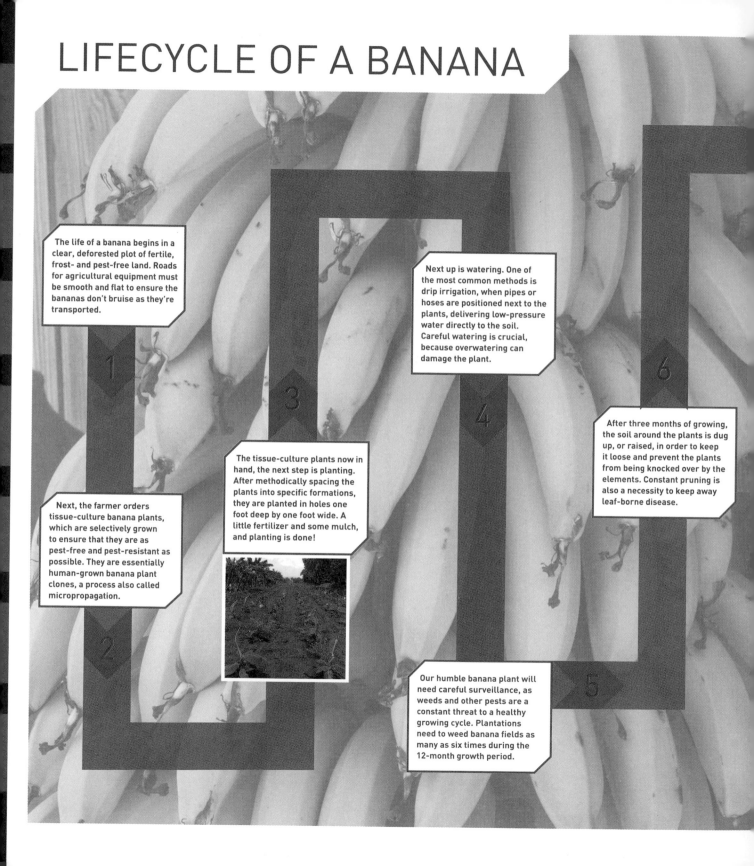

1 The life of a banana begins in a clear, deforested plot of fertile, frost- and pest-free land. Roads for agricultural equipment must be smooth and flat to ensure the bananas don't bruise as they're transported.

2 Next, the farmer orders tissue-culture banana plants, which are selectively grown to ensure that they are as pest-free and pest-resistant as possible. They are essentially human-grown banana plant clones, a process also called micropropagation.

3 The tissue-culture plants now in hand, the next step is planting. After methodically spacing the plants into specific formations, they are planted in holes one foot deep by one foot wide. A little fertilizer and some mulch, and planting is done!

4 Next up is watering. One of the most common methods is drip irrigation, when pipes or hoses are positioned next to the plants, delivering low-pressure water directly to the soil. Careful watering is crucial, because overwatering can damage the plant.

5 Our humble banana plant will need careful surveillance, as weeds and other pests are a constant threat to a healthy growing cycle. Plantations need to weed banana fields as many as six times during the 12-month growth period.

6 After three months of growing, the soil around the plants is dug up, or raised, in order to keep it loose and prevent the plants from being knocked over by the elements. Constant pruning is also a necessity to keep away leaf-borne disease.

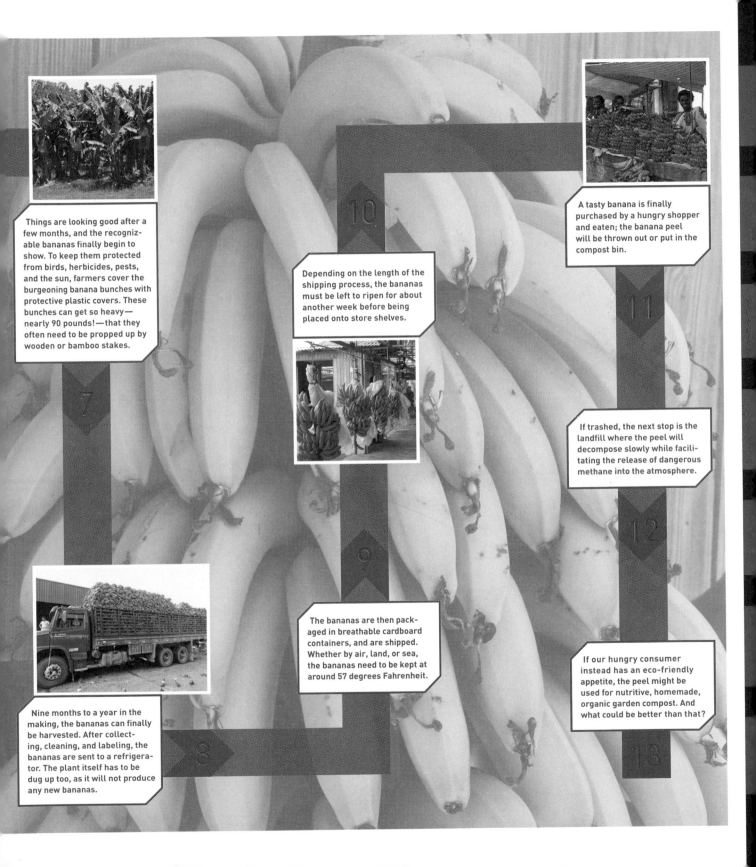

7 Things are looking good after a few months, and the recognizable bananas finally begin to show. To keep them protected from birds, herbicides, pests, and the sun, farmers cover the burgeoning banana bunches with protective plastic covers. These bunches can get so heavy—nearly 90 pounds!—that they often need to be propped up by wooden or bamboo stakes.

10 Depending on the length of the shipping process, the bananas must be left to ripen for about another week before being placed onto store shelves.

11 A tasty banana is finally purchased by a hungry shopper and eaten; the banana peel will be thrown out or put in the compost bin.

12 If trashed, the next stop is the landfill where the peel will decompose slowly while facilitating the release of dangerous methane into the atmosphere.

8 Nine months to a year in the making, the bananas can finally be harvested. After collecting, cleaning, and labeling, the bananas are sent to a refrigerator. The plant itself has to be dug up too, as it will not produce any new bananas.

9 The bananas are then packaged in breathable cardboard containers, and are shipped. Whether by air, land, or sea, the bananas need to be kept at around 57 degrees Fahrenheit.

13 If our hungry consumer instead has an eco-friendly appetite, the peel might be used for nutritive, homemade, organic garden compost. And what could be better than that?

CITRUS PEEL CANDLES

Citrus peels are a fun way to make beautiful, organic candles. Don't stop at just one — create a group of them as a centerpiece for your next holiday table. For ages 12 and up.

WHAT YOU NEED

- Citrus fruits
- Candlewicks
- Old candles
- Knife
- Tin can
- Old pan
- Stove or hotplate
- Pliers

TIP: CLEMENTINE ORANGES ARE ESPECIALLY GOOD TO USE BECAUSE THE SKIN EASILY PEELS AWAY.

Cut the citrus in half. Carefully squeeze out the juice of each half into a bowl — you don't want to tear the skin; set the juice aside (you can enjoy it later as a refreshing beverage). Scoop out any of the pith and flesh left inside the peel.

Place the tea light wick into the center of the peel.

Heat up your candle wax using an old pan and a tin can.

Once your wax is melted, remove the can from the heat with pliers. Pour the wax into the citrus peels, making sure that the wick stays centered. Let wax set.

I really wonder what gives us the right to wreck this poor planet of ours.
— KURT VONNEGUT

A typical household in the U.S. generates about 650 pounds of compostable waste annually.

Heaven is under our feet as well as over our heads.

— HENRY DAVID THOREAU, *Walden*

If you like buying organic food, try buying locally grown as often as possible—the food will be fresher and it isn't traveling long distances (all that transportation is bad for the environment).

RESOURCES

These are some of our favorite books and websites. For a full list of sources of facts and figures in the book, please visit TerraCycle.com.

BOOKS

Braungart, Michael, and William McDonough. *Cradle to Cradle: Remaking the Way We Make Things.* New York: North Point Press, 2002.

Carson, Rachel. *Silent Spring.* New York: Fawcett Crest Books, 1962. Paperback reprint edition, New York: Houghton Mifflin Company, 2002.

Cline, Elizabeth. *Overdressed: The Shockingly High Cost of Cheap Fashion.* New York: Portfolio Hardcover, 2012.

Dorfman, Josh. *The Lazy Environmentalist on a Budget: Save Money. Save Time. Save the Planet.* New York: Stewart, Tabori and Chang, 2009.

Friedman, Thomas L. *Hot, Flat, & Crowded: Why We Need a Green Revolution—and How It Can Renew America.* New York: Farrar, Straus and Giroux, 2008.

Gore, Al. *An Inconvenient Truth.* New York: Rodale Press, 2006.

Hawken, Paul, Amory Lovins, and L. Hunter Lovins. *Natural Capitalism: Creating the Next Industrial Revolution.* Boston: Little, Brown, and Company, 1999.

Hirshberg, Gary. *Stirring It Up: How to Make Money and Save the World.* New York: Hyperion, 2008.

Moore, Kathleen Dean, and Michael P. Nelson. *Moral Ground: Ethical Action for a Planet in Peril.* San Antonion, Texas: Trinity University Press, 2010.

Pollan, Michael. *The Omnivore's Dilemma: A Natural History of Four Meals.* New York: Penguin, 2007.

Szaky, Tom. *Outsmart Waste: The Modern Idea of Garbage and How to Think Our Way Out of It.* San Francisco: Berrett-Koehler Publishers, 2014.

WEBSITES

1-800-Recycling
1800recycling.com

Alliance for Green Heat
forgreenheat.org

The Daily Green Newsletter
goodhousekeeping.com/home/green-living/the-daily-green

Earth911
earth911.com

Engineers Without Borders
ewb-usa.org

Previous: An urban landfill overflowing with garbage. //
Opposite: TerraCycle's testing facility in New Jersey.

Ethical Fashion Forum: SOURCE Database
ethicalfashionforum.com/source

Food Pantries
foodpantries.org

Freitag
freitag.ch

Gardener's Supply Company
gardeners.com

GoodGuide
goodguide.com

Green Map System
greenmap.org

Grist
grist.org

Habitat for Humanity: Material Donations
habitat.org/getinv/materials_donations.aspx

Keep America Beautiful
kab.org

Poo Poo Paper
new.poopoopaper.com

Recycle-A-Bulb
recycleabulb.com

Recycle Across America
recycleacrossamerica.org

Reuse Everything Institute
reuseeverything.org

Solving the E-Waste Problem (StEP)
step-initiative.org

TreeHugger
treehugger.com

We Hate to Waste
wehatetowaste.com

PHOTO CREDITS

MAKE GARBAGE GREAT

HarperCollins books may be purchased for educational, business, or sales promotional use. For information please e-mail the Special Markets Department at SPsales@ harpercollins.com.

First published in 2015 by
Harper Design
An Imprint of HarperCollins*Publishers*

195 Broadway
New York, NY 10007
Tel: (212) 207-7000
Fax: (855) 746-6023
www.hc.com
harperdesign@harpercollins.com

Distributed throughout the world by
HarperCollins*Publishers*
195 Broadway
New York, NY 10007

ISBN 978-0-06-234885-2

Library of Congress Control Number: 2014930209

Book design by: Galen Smith / Hardscrabble Projects

Printed in China
First Printing, 2015

ABOUT THE AUTHORS

TOM SZAKY is the founder and CEO of TerraCycle, an international leader in the collection and repurposing of hard-to-recycle post-consumer waste, from used chip bags to cigarette butts. On a yearly basis and across 23 countries, TerraCycle collects and repurposes billions of pieces of waste, creating millions of dollars of donations for schools and charities in the process. Many of the world's largest consumer product companies contract with TerraCycle to collect and recycle post-consumer products and packaging. Through TerraCycle, Tom has pioneered a process, involving manufacturers, retailers, consumers, and community groups, to create circular solutions for waste that otherwise would go to landfills or be incinerated.

Tom is the author of two other books, *Revolution in a Bottle* (April 2009) and *Outsmart Waste* (January 2014). He is an acclaimed international public speaker, making presentations to corporate and academic audiences regularly. Tom created, produces, and stars in a new reality TV show, *Human Resources,* currently airing on Pivot TV. Tom and TerraCycle have received more than 100 social, environmental, and business awards from a range of organizations including the United Nations, World Economic Forum, and the Environmental Protection Agency.

ALBE ZAKES is the Global Vice President of Marketing & Communications for TerraCycle. Albe was integral in transforming TerraCycle from a small startup into a successful and highly visible recycling innovator that runs pre- and post-consumer packaging reclamation programs for major manufacturers such as Kraft Foods, Frito-Lay, L'Oreal, 3M, Kimberly-Clark, Proctor & Gamble, and Newell Rubbermaid. PR News named Albe one of its Rising Stars of PR in 2012 and Social Media MVP in 2014; he received Cause Marketing Forum's Golden Halo Award in 2013. Albe also manages, stars in, and produces TerraCycle's Pivot TV show, *Human Resources*. He writes and edits the company's blogs and columns for major publications including the *New York Times Magazine*, *TreeHugger*, *Sustainable Brands*, and *Huffington Post*.

JERRY GREENFIELD and his longtime friend and business partner Ben Cohen are the men behind one of the most talked about and least conventional success stories in American business. Cofounder of Ben & Jerry's Homemade, Inc., Jerry has helped to build a storefront venture into an ice cream and business marvel by making social responsibility and creative management strengths, rather than weaknesses. He and Ben have received the James Beard Humanitarians of the Year and the Peace Museum's Community Peacemakers of the Year awards. Presently, Jerry is involved in promoting the social and environmental initiatives that Ben & Jerry's undertakes. He is also president of the Ben & Jerry's Foundation.